RECIPES IN PERPETUITY

Timeless Tastes and Tales

from

Residents and Future Residents of Mount Holly

Compiled by

Frances Anderson Cranford

Nancy Nixon McDonough

and

Mary Fletcher Worthen

Patricia Kelly Freeman, designer

Dedication

This book is dedicated to Mary Worthen, without whom it would not have been possible. Mary's sharp mind, wit, and unique knowledge of the history and residents of Mount Holly guided us in the research and gathering of tales and recipes for the book. Of course, she would have liked for all of the residents to be included, but time and space were limited. Mary's commitment to Mount Holly has been shown through her service on the Mount Holly Cemetery Association Board since 1951.

CONTENTS

INTRODUCTION

America is a nation of immigrants who arrived, mastered a new language and culture, and lived successful and productive lives that enriched our nation.

In Arkansas, many of those early settlers—and others like them through the years—rest in Mount Holly Cemetery.

To share our love for Mount Holly, we have composed this cookbook as an ode to its inhabitants. Inside are the stories of many who are buried here and, as southern women have always shared their recipes—passing them around and passing them down—we are passing along some favorite recipes of Mount Holly residents and future residents.

Please enjoy, and please come to visit.

ABOUT MOUNT HOLLY

With early burials scattered in various places, the city of Little Rock badly needed a public burying ground. The problem was solved in 1843 when two of the leading citizens donated a four block square on the "outskirts of the city," held a picnic on the land in May, and auctioned off the original lots. (That first picnic is commemorated with the annual Mount Holly Picnic.) Since the beginning the cemetery has remained the same size, but has grown into one of the most beautiful cemeteries in the country.

Thousands of visitors come each year for various reasons. Those interested in history (including many groups of school children) come to see the resting places of the earliest citizens of the state and of twelve state governors, five U.S. Senators, five Confederate generals, black artisans, and a Cherokee princess. For others the cemetery is an open air museum of artistic eras, Classical, Victoran, Art Deco, Modern, all expressed in gravestone styles from simple to elaborate. Some come to read the epitaphs that range from heart breaking to humorous to mysterious.

As the roses have covered the surrounding fences and the trees have grown to shade the graves, the cemetery has become a place of peace. Benches are placed throughout for the contemplation of the overall beauty and the study of funerary symbols such as the side by side columns, covered with a single stone pall and bound together by a tasseled rope, signifying a couple united in life and now forever together; Gabriel with his untried horn; the willow tree, a symbol of immortality; the wreath symbolizing victory over death; the reversed torches signifying the snuffing out of life; and the cross and anchor—symbol of salvation. Angels, Celtic crosses, and hands pointing heavenward join the cherubs on the graves of the many young children lost in those early years. There are stones telling the stories of people's lives—the young firefighter killed in the line of duty who stands proudly in his uniform, the tree trunks for the Woodmen of the World, and the various symbols indicating war service and brotherhoods. All are there to remind us of the fascinating persons who have gone before us and whose interments have caused Mount Holly to be called "The Westminster Abbey of Arkansas."

Today the cemetery is maintained by the Mount Holly Cemetery Association, a non-profit organization with a volunteer Board of Directors. This group oversees the grounds, the rock walls and fences that surround the cemetery, the charming bell house, the historically accurate sexton's house, and the receiving house - along with all the duties that are involved in caring for such an important piece of our country's history. In this endeavor they are blessed with a caring and capable sexton who manages all of the property with devotion. In the early 1990s, the Pulaski County Master Gardeners adopted Mount Holly Cemetery as one of their projects to help maintain with volunteer labor. Among the projects that they have undertaken at Mount Holly is restoring the plantings around the perimeter with New Dawn roses.

The cemetery is located at 12th and Broadway Streets in Little Rock, Arkansas. Gates are open from 8 a.m. until 5 p.m. in the summer and from 8 a.m. until 4 p.m. in the winter. The gate on Broadway is closed in inclement weather.

Mount Holly Special Events

One of the most joyous events at Mount Holly is a tour of the cemetery by a group of school children. This happens throughout the school year with classes coming from all over the state. Students receive lessons in history, art, and respect for those who have gone before; and they often write thank you notes to the Mount Holly volunteer who has guided them through the cemetery. They find the mausoleum "cool," David O. Dodd's grave interesting, and are fasci- nated by the story of the statues representing the two young sisters. Sometimes their comments and the pictures they draw on their notes bring a smile to our faces:

David O. Dodd

"I never knew that there were so many ways to bury a dead body." "The mausoleum was also very cool. I enjoyed walking in it and looking at how old people were when they died." "I have always enjoyed cemeteries; but Mount Holly has been the best I've been to by far. I mostly enjoyed the story of the two daughters who were made into statues." "I learned about the cremations buried under the water fountain. It really makes me think about doing the same thing when I die." And finally: "Knowing that some important Arkansans are buried there makes Arkansas seem less lame."

Other special events include the "Tales of the Crypt" every fall, presented by drama students at Parkview Arts-Science Magnet High School, First Presbyterian Church, and the Mount Holly Cemetery Association. The students write their own scripts and, in period costumes, portray historical residents.

Another popular event is the annual Spring Picnic and Fair on the last Sunday in April. In addition to the delicious box supper, there are tours, a silent auction, and a variety of crafts and other items for sale to raise money for the maintenance of the cemetery.

WELCOME!

My friends, it is indeed a pleasure To welcome you in stately measure
Like that in which the great Cutullus Replied to that far famed Lucullus,
He who was history's greatest eater Yet never saw a biscuit beater.
But all this is beyond the question The Latin word for indigestion
We promise not to even mention. Nor conjugation or declension.
Because we want to make you happy, We'll make this short and snappy.
We are glad to have you here tonight And hope you brought your appetite.

This welcome to the final (and only) banquet of the Latin Club at East Side Junior High School in 1932 was written for Mary Fletcher (Worthen) by her Godfather, Bob Butterfield. Mary thought this part of it would be a great welcome 78 years later to the Mount Holly cookbook.

Beverages

ÆSTHETIC
CLVB

"Come spend the afternoon with me next Tuesday," invited Mrs. Rufus Julius Polk (Hallie Woodruff). And with four neighbors and friends she started The Aesthetic Club on January 16, 1883. The ladies were in their 20s and 30s and wanted to form a club, but realized they were inexperienced and so they asked Mrs. Gilbert Knapp, age 58, to guide them. Oscar Wilde had recently made a trip to the United States promoting Gilbert and Sullivan's operettas, especially *Patience*, and the aesthetic movement in general, so Mrs. Knapp suggested the name Aesthetic Club.

Women's clubs were just beginning all over the country, and The Aesthetic Club was one of the first in Arkansas and west of the Mississippi. It provided the opportunity for like-minded friends to meet for a "feast of reason" where no refreshments were served and the topics of children, servants, and ages were prohibited. The idea was immediately popular; and the membership grew to one hundred by 1895, where it remains today.

At first they met in homes restricted to east of Main Street because few of the women had carriages and had to walk wherever they went. They outgrew their homes; but several members were on the Columbian Exposition committee, and when that was over artifacts were displayed in the Arsenal building and members of the Aesthetic Club were invited to meet there in the Columbian Room. Meetings are held twice a month "to present programs of literary, artistic, musical, and timely trends." Their motto is "The Good, the True, and the Beautiful;" and their slogan is "Innocently to amuse, the imagination in this dream of life is wisdom." Some people think the reason the club has lasted so long is the rule that papers are limited to 15 minutes—even if the assigned paper is "the history of the world, from the beginning to the sixteenth century."

The club still meets in the Arsenal and has had a lot to do with the building's preservation, especially during the Great Depression. The papers are even better than they used to be; and the members still have a good time and still do not do any "good works."

Church Punch

1 gallon pineapple sherbet   2 bottles Ginger Ale (more, if needed)

Mix and serve.

Rum–Tea Punch

2 cups lemon juice   1 $^{1}/_{2}$ cups amber rum   1 cup strong tea

$^{1}/_{2}$ cup brandy   2 cups superfine sugar   2 lemons, thinly sliced and seeded

8 cups cold water

In a large bowl combine lemon juice, tea, sugar, and cold water. Stir until well blended. Add rum, brandy, and lemon slices. More rum, brandy or lemon juice mixture can be added, according to taste. Pour over ice ring in a punch bowl. (To make an ice ring, freeze lemon and orange slices interspersed with mint sprigs in a ring mold.) Makes 2 dozen 4-ounce punch cups.

Refreshing Drink

White grape juice   Ginger ale   Fresh strawberries

Freeze mint in ice cubes, Mix ginger ale and juice (half & half). Pour over ice in glass putting strawberry on top.

Fruit Punch

3 cups cranberry juice cocktail   1 (1-liter) bottle ginger ale, chilled   2 cups pineapple juice

$^{3}/_{4}$ to 1 cup light rum (if desired)   2 cups orange juice

Combine the three juices in a large bowl, and chill up to 8 hours, if desired. Stir ginger ale and rum into juice mixture just before serving. Serve over ice.

THE BOATHOUSE, officially The Athletic Association of Little Rock, was started in 1882. Water sports had been talked about since the early 1870's; and finally in a meeting at the Capital Hotel a plan was formulated to provide opportunities for physical development for businessmen, for regattas, and also row boats for individual members to "have a quiet pull along the river after the moon is up." The clubhouse, on the river next to Main Street, was finished in June, complete with indoor plumbing. The *Arkansas Gazette* of June 30, 1882, printed this item: "Hugh Barclay, they say, stands under its shower bath and recites touching and eloquent passages from Romeo and Juliet."

The first regatta was held in 1883, and they took place almost every year afterward—on the 4th of July, and in later years on Labor Day. The barges raced from the Baring Cross Bridge to the Main Street Bridge. The oarsmen had female sponsors and maids, and the regattas were important social events through the years.

The building burned in 1887 but was immediately replaced with a better one finished in 1889. "Dr." John Beidelman, a pharmacist fondly called Dr., served as president from 1883 until 1895. Later presidents served only one, or maybe two years. The club was closed during World War I, when officers were billeted there, and also in the first years of the Depression. It resumed regattas in 1932 and continued through 1936. There was no regatta in 1937 because of the looming war; but the clubhouse was open until the early morning of April 13, 1938, when it burned to the ground. No one could determine the cause of the fire.

Member Archie House wrote: "With the advent of country clubs, automobiles, and modern hotels with large ballrooms, the importance of the Boathouse dwindled." There was no yearning for restoration—only a fond farewell to an organization which had flourished in its day, had served the city's needs, and had brought immeasurable pleasure to its members and their guests."

The Rudder, the club's newsletter started in 1924, was published irregularly until the fire. It contained news of the members and corny jokes, such as: "Dear Mr. Louder'—My wife insists on naming our baby girl Opium. I wonder why? Fond Papa. Dear Pop—the dictionary says opium comes from a wild poppy; and you know yourself better than I do, so figure it for yourself. Ring."

A History of Punch

Punch was first tasted in India by British sailors in the 1630s. The five basic ingredients were water, citrus, alcohol, spices, and sugar; and it was called "panch." The ingredients and proportions varied; but it could be mixed in advance and served hot or cold.

The sailors liked it so much that they took the idea back with them to Great Britain; and its popularity spread across Europe and to the American colonies.

Because of its potency, it was at first a drink only for the men to enjoy—at home, in taverns, or in gentlemen's clubs. Occasionally, it was served in the presence of women; and they came to love it too, especially on holidays and other festive occasions.

THE EDELWEISS, a women's study club, was started in 1895 with the limitation of fifteen members. They meet once a month, October through May. Generally, there are no refreshments; but the first and last meetings they have a box lunch and there is a luncheon at the December meeting.

Their mottos are "We shall not pass this way again" and "It is much better to understand little than to misunderstand much." Some members are the third generation.

Fish House Punch

1 Fifth lemon or lime juice

1 cup sugar

1 Fifth water

2 Fifths Jamaican rum

1 Fifth brandy

1 cup peach brandy

2 peaches, peeled and sliced

In a bowl, empty the rum and brandy bottles and use one for measuring water and lime juice. Dissolve the sugar in the water and stir in the lemon or lime juice. Mix in the other ingredients. Allow the mixture to mellow for a few hours, or overnight, before using. In order to keep dilution to a minimum, chill the mixture thoroughly before pouring it over a good-sized chunk of ice in a punch bowl. Garnish with peaches. Serves approximately 40 4-oz. punch glasses. Note: A good rum to use is a mixture of 75 percent to 80 percent Light or Golden Rum, and 20 to 25 percent Myers Jamaica Rum. Double the water content if a less potent punch is preferred, but always allow for the melting of the ice.

A potent, traditional punch originating with men of a hunting and fishing club in 1732.

Gilt Edge Hunting and Fishing Club

In 1880, four men met at Dr. James Edwin Gibson's drug store (northeast corner of Main and Markham) to organize a hunting and fishing club. It soon grew to eight members and was named the Gilt Edge Hunting and Fishing Club because it boasted a silver service donated by James H. Hornibrook. The owner of a tavern, Mr. Hornibrook had saved mutilated silver coins and had them made into silver cups and plates like everyday tin ones. Each member had his name engraved on the flatware.

In a few years some younger men formed a similar club and called themselves the N. L. Club, which they said stood for "No Lying."

The Gilt Edges invited, in 1887, the N.L.s to join them in a fishing trip to the Ouachita River. They had no clubhouse; they just pitched a large tent at different places for their trips. On this excursion, Dr. Gibson took a picture of the combined clubs with one of the first cameras in Arkansas. From this small round snapshot, less than three inches in diameter, he had his sister, Maria, paint a picture 37" by 25"; and the men are recognizable (opposite page). He gave the painting to the Gilt Edge Club; but when everyone wanted it, they raffled it off and J. A. Woodson won. When he died his widow gave it to Dr. Gibson.

The silver service was to go to the last survivor, who was James G. Woodson, a little boy who subsequently died. He was the son of James A. Woodson. What is left now belongs to Robert W. Duffy of St. Louis, great grandson of Woodson. He wrote: "My great uncle Jack was a black sheep, to say the least. He sold a bunch of stuff, and it is amazing that this silver escaped his trips to the pawnshop. He leapt to his reward from either the Main Street or the Broadway Bridge."

THE GILT EDGE CLUB:

Dr. A. L. Breysacher*	J.A. Woodson*	W. H. Wilson	Frank Botsford*
James Hornibrook*	Joe Griffith*	Dr. James E. Gibson*	Augustus H. Garland*

THE N. L. CLUB:

Dr. James A. Dibrell*	Booker Worthen*	Frank T. Gibson	Dr. Lorenzo P. Gibson*
Horace Booker*	Clay Jones		

*Buried at Mount Holly

The Gilt Edge Hunting and Fishing Club and the N. L. Club—this painting was commissioned by Dr. James Dibrell and features him standing in the forefront. The original painting is hanging today in a Quapaw Quarter home.

Red Sangria

¹/₃ red wine   ¹/₃ orange juice   ¹/₆ brandy   ¹/₆ Cointreau   Raspberries

Mix in pitcher. Serve over ice and enjoy.

White Sangria

¹/₂ gal. Chablis white wine (not Rhine wine)
1 cup Curaçao (orange flavored liquer)
¹/₂ cup sugar

Slice 1 lemon, 1 lime, and 1 orange. Cut slices in half and add to above mixture. Cool in refrigerator for at least 1 hour, but it can be kept for a week.

Add 20 oz. club soda just before serving.

THE HALLIE RIFLES were announced in the *Arkansas Gazette* in 1874 as being reorganized, saying that "their muster roll bears the names of 70 of the very best young men of our city. Their armory, located in the Dodge block at the corner of Scott and Markham Streets, is being put in perfect order. The regular nights for drill are Fridays for the full company and Saturday for officers." The company was named for Hallie Jabine (Mrs. Claude H. Sayle). The steamboat Hallie, that had a prominent part in the Brooks-Baxter war, was also named for her.

THE FLETCHER RIFLES, organized in 1890, were named for John Gould Fletcher, Sr., who generously but modestly offered to uniform the company. At their first drill in Indianapolis on the 4th of July 1891, they won second prize. They organized a Zouave team and took it to the World's Fair in St. Louis in 1893. There were 38 enlisted men and four officers. Their motto was "Perseverantia omnia vincet."

French Iced Coffee

4 ¹/₂ cups strong coffee
3 tsp. vanilla
24 oz. half & half
1 ¹/₂ qts. milk
3 cups sugar

Dissolve sugar in hot coffee. Cool. Add other ingredients. Pour into milk cartons to freeze. Remove from freezer 2 hours before serving. Mix & serve very icy. Makes 27 cups.

THE WOMEN'S EMERGENCY COMMITTEE was organized when Governor Orval Faubus closed all the public high schools in Little Rock in 1958 to avoid token integration.

These women grew in number to 1,400. Many were happy with segregation but valued education even more. They labored hard for a year, including working to get moderates elected to the school board, and managed to get the schools open early in August, 1959. They inspired some women from their group, who called themselves the Panel of American Women, to travel around the state to help people accept integration. This panel—which included a Protestant, a Jew, an African American, a Roman Catholic, and a leader—would give programs promoting equality in everyday living by showing the lack of it. They accomplished their goal in five years.

Women's Emergency Committee to Open Our Schools members Vivion L. Brewer, Adolphine Fletcher Terry, and Pat House (left to right); November 2, 1963.

Courtesy of the Butler Center for Arkansas Studies, Central Arkansas Library System

GERTRUDE REMMEL BUTLER* (Mrs. Richard C. Butler) had many firsts. She was the first female cheerleader and in the first graduating class of Little Rock High School (now Central High) in 1928. Gertie, as she was called by friends, won many trophies for archery and became a model for Ben Pearson bows and arrows. She volunteered and supported many local and state non-profits throughout her life and won many first place ribbons in flower shows. The Gertrude Remmel Butler Child Development Center at First United Methodist Church was established in her honor.

RICHARD C. BUTLER—a lawyer, banker, investor and developer—was a leader in the state's industrial development and cultural preservation. Serving in World War II in the China-Burma-India theater of war, he was awarded the Bronze Star. He was known as a man of unflinching integrity. His hobby was horticulture; and he was famous for his hybridized daffodils, irises, and daylilies. The Butler Center for Arkansas Studies was established in his memory.

*The names of residents of Mt. Holly (those buried there), if not identified elsewhere, will appear in all capital letters.

Wassail Bowl

¹⁄₂ cup sugar	2" stick cinnamon	1 qt. sweet cider
¹⁄₂ cup water	1¹⁄₂ qt. orange juice	1 orange, sliced thin
12 cloves	2 cups grapefruit juice	

Simmer sugar, water, and spices 10 minutes. Add remainder and reheat.
Serves 25.

Spirited Wassail

1 gal. apple cider	10 2" cinnamon sticks	¹⁄₂ pt. brandy
1¹⁄₂ cups lemon juice	1 qt. vodka	2 oranges, sliced
		(stuck with cloves)

Heat to boil and add liquor.

JAMES H. HORNIBROOK was born in Toronto June 8, 1840, married MARGARET R. MCCULLY in 1863, and came to Little Rock in 1867. He was in the Spanish American War, and a member of the Gilt Edge Hunting and Fishing Club, the Knights of Pythias, the Defiance Hook and Ladder Company, and was a successful liquor dealer. He built a wonderful turreted house at 22nd and Louisiana Streets, which still stands as The Empress bed and breakfast. (Opposite page.)

After supper on May 24, 1890, he went downtown to his saloon and had a delightful time with friends. They broke up at about 3:00 a.m.; and four of them boarded the street car home, getting off at 22nd and Main Streets. They parted, going in different directions. To the young man, an employee, who lived across the street, he said, "Goodnight, my boy," his last words. He went through the front gate, got the house keys out of his pocket, and collapsed on the sidewalk. It was not until 6 o'clock that a butcher boy, delivering orders, found him. According to Dr. Gibson, he died instantly of a stroke. The newspaper noted that he had a $3,000 life insurance policy.

Gilt Edge Hunting Club silver

Nana's Eggnog

Beat 12 egg yolks (must be fresh and at room temp.)

Slowly add 6 Tbs. sugar—beat until fluffy.

Slowly add 12 oz. bourbon and 4 oz. rum and set aside.

Beat 12 egg whites and finally add 6 Tbs. sugar until very stiff.

Fold together and serve immediately in cut glass glasses. Nutmeg on the side.

Toasted pecans may be offered, but nothing else because of the approaching dinner.

In the 1880's Lena Fischer Hagan served Nana's Eggnog at 11:00 a.m. on Christmas morning (between church service and dinner) at 1013 West 3rd St. In the 1950's her granddaughter Mildred Hornibrook Harrison was still serving the same recipe to family and friends.

When Lena died, her son J.T. Hornibrook and his son Jimmie moved in with Mildred and Pup Harrison. J.T. drove a square black Chevy which he would race down the driveway and screech in a tight curve to approach the garage. Mildred shook her head and said, "He used to drive the buggy like that, too."

EDWIN B. CROMWELL, a distinguished architect and leader in the historical preservation community, was an especially good friend of Mount Holly. He supervised the restoration of the "Receiving House" (where bodies were kept until burial), a 12 by 15 foot structure that was over 125 years old and leaning at a critical angle. After making it level and plumb, the new foundations, floor, and wall framing were constructed. Old, weathered boards were found to replace some of the original siding. It was lifted on props during the restoration, and Ed remarked that it was the first time he had built a structure from the top down.

Ed Cromwell's Eggnog

6 eggs, separated (beaten separately)   1 lb. sugar (1 ½ cups)   2 pints XX cream, whipped
1 pint Bourbon whiskey   (½ pint Jamaican Rum)

Beat yolks well. Add sugar gradually. Beat until smooth and creamy. Add whiskey and mix well. (Sugar must be well dissolved before adding whiskey.) Then add whipped whites of eggs. Add whipped cream. (The next morning, add rum.)

Ed Cromwell adapted this from an old Watkins-Thompson family recipe.

Receiving House

Crease Family Eggnog

(Transcribed from a recipe card of Jane Pollard Newton Crease.)

6 dozen eggs, beaten separately   1 heaping Tbs. (per egg) sugar

1 1/2 to 2 quarts Whiskey

Beat egg yolks very light. Add sugar and continue to beat until sugar is dissolved and mixture is very light in texture and pale yellow in color. Add liquor slowly, continuing to beat. Fold in beaten whites and serve at once.

On the back of the card is this note: "If you want to fix one portion for a sick person –

> 1 egg
>
> 1 Tbs. sugar
>
> 1 jigger whiskey
>
> Enough milk or cream to fill small water glass."

JANE CREASE (1798-1872) was married at age 15 to JOHN CREASE with whom she lived as wife for 58 years. They moved to Arkansas in 1837 when John received the appointment of Cashier of the Bank of the State of Arkansas. He later was elected as Treasurer of the State. They first resided in Little Rock, then settled on a farm in Saline County that they named "Retirement," a place which soon earned a widespread reputation for generous hospitality. She was the mother of ten children; and, according to a newspaper article written at the time of her death, "It was her lot to be left a mother to many who were left motherless in this world, and kindly did she lighten that heaviest of all loads that ever yet befell the young." We can only imagine what this large family's Christmas celebrations were like, with this potion as a centerpiece.

Alice Campbell's Eggnog

Beat separately the yolks and whites of 6 eggs. Add ½ cup sugar to the yolks while beating and ¼ cup sugar to the whites after they have been beaten stiff. Mix the whites and yolks gently, then stir in 1 pint rich cream and 1 pint milk. Add 1 pint whiskey and 1 ounce rum.

In modern times, be warned that the eggs are raw in this recipe, but generations have partaken with no harm—perhaps due to the large amount of alcohol, which may have sterilized any germ bold enough to appear.

A Latin teacher who brought the dead language to life and made it exciting was FRANCES VINSONHALER WILLIAMS. She was fondly remembered by her students. One day her students put a sign above her door at school that said, "Abandon hope, all ye that enter here." It was that year that the school dedicated its yearbook to her.

Milk Punch

| 1 cup ice | 16 oz. milk | 4 oz. bourbon |
| ½ cup powdered sugar | 1 ½ tsp. vanilla | Nutmeg |

Pour in blender and blend on high.
Top with sprinkled nutmeg.

This is a Vinsonhaler family recipe. One Christmas when neighbors were invited to a traditional milk punch party, a teetotalling, quiet, reserved lady got very rosy drinking her punch and in all seriousness asked, "Where does one get such a cow? I want this cow."

HUGH B. PATTERSON was part of a small but influential minority who bucked generations of history to work for an end to legal segregation. He was publisher of the *Arkansas Gazette* in 1957 when the newspaper took a stand against segregated schools during a federal-state confrontation. By supporting desegregation, the *Gazette* suffered severe losses in advertising and circulation.

Patterson and his wife at that time, Louise, had to persuade her father Mr. J. N. Heiskell, the editor, that his grandchildren should not have to grow up in a racially unjust society. For its coverage of the confrontation, the *Gazette* was awarded a Pulitzer Prize for public service and another for editorials written by Harry Ashmore. The paper also received a Freedom House award.

Under Patterson's financial leadership the paper, with losses amounting to a million or more, recovered the losses and set records in circulation and advertising. And the *Gazette* became a magnet for bright young journalists.

Having been publisher for 38 years, Patterson left the *Gazette* shortly after it was sold to Gannett Company, Inc. in 1986. Founded in 1819, the *Gazette* was closed in 1991 and merged with the *Arkansas Democrat* after years of fierce competition.

After Dinner Drink

$^1/_2$ gal. vanilla ice cream

1 oz. triple sec

2 oz. crème de menthe

1 oz. white crème de cacao

Put in blender and blend. Serve in champagne glasses.

Velvet Hammer

1 jigger crème de cocao	1 jigger brandy
1 jigger Cointreau	1 qt. ice cream

Blend in electric blender and serve in stemmed glasses. Double for 6 – 8.

Brandy Ice

1 qt. vanilla ice cream	4 jiggers brandy
2 jiggers Cointreau	

Blend in electric blender and serve in stemmed glasses.

Mary Worthen's Mint Tea

Steep family-size tea bag in boiling water for about 5 minutes. In another container steep 6-8 sprigs of fresh mint in boiling water for about 15 minutes.

Combine the above and add 1 cup sugar. Add $1/2$ cup lemon juice. Stir. Add water to make about 2 quarts.

Mount Holly Wine Spritzer

Mix white wine and lemonade (half & half) with fresh mint and serve over ice.

(This refreshing drink was created at our first Mount Holly fundraising picnic and remains a favorite.)

"The Mount Holly cemetery may seem like an unlikely tourist destination, but thousands tramp around its headstones every year, seeking out the graves of an Indian chief's wife and the boy martyr of the Confederacy. The 166-year old cemetery also draws those looking for the final resting places of early politicians and residents whose names are now attached to Arkansas counties ... (It) is listed in the city's list of Top 12 spots tourists must see on a trip to Little Rock." *—Arkansas Democrat Gazette,* 25 June, 2009

Appetizers

THE HERB SOCIETY was organized in 1966 and accepted as the Arkansas Unit of the Herb Society of America at that time. The HSA, as it is referred to, was started in Massachusetts in 1933, the very bottom of the Great Depression. Herbs had almost been forgotten along the way, so there was a lot of work to do. Arkansas, by providing three public gardens—the Garden of Exploration at the Arkansas School for the Blind, the Medicinal Garden at Historic Arkansas Museum, and the Herb Garden at the Governor's Mansion—helped spread the word. HSA members continue to maintain these herb gardens.

The Garden of Exploration contains not only herbs but, since some legally blind people can see colors, some bright flowers have been added there. Most of the herbs in the Medicinal Garden are also used in cooking, but their medicinal use is more interesting. The Herb Garden at the Governor's Mansion is mostly culinary, and the chefs there use the many herbs.

Most herbs need a lot of sun—at least four or five hours each day—and they all need good drainage and only moderately rich soil. The most popular ones are chives, parsley, basil, French sorrel, fennel, mint, thyme, and the Mediterranean herbs: French lavender, rosemary, and oregano. Most herbs may be planted from seed but rosemary roots easier from cuttings. Fresh herbs are better than dried, but they may be dried in a dark place and kept bone dry in a screw top jar.

Herb Spread

4 (3 oz.) pkgs. cream cheese, softened
1 Tbs. chopped chives
1 tsp. chopped fresh parsley
2 Tbs. butter, softened
2 Tbs. dried dillweed (4 Tbs. fresh)
$\frac{1}{4}$ tsp. garlic powder

Combine all ingredients, mixing well. Spoon mixture into a covered container. Chill at least 1 hour or until ready to use. Yield: about 1$\frac{1}{2}$ cups.

Herbed Yogurt Cheese

1 quart plain yogurt   Lemon juice
1 1/2 cups chopped herbs (parsley, chives, thyme, basil, oregano, etc.)

Place yogurt in cheesecloth-lined sieve and weight with plate and heavy object on top. Refrigerate over night. Throw away the whey or use to make bread. Place cheese in bowl, add lemon juice to taste. Add herbs, mix well, refrigerate for three hours to bring out flavor. Use as you would any soft cheese.

Entrance to Governor's Mansion Herb Garden

Mediterranean Torte Appetizer

Cooking oil spray to coat mini-loaf pan

$^1/_4$ cup prepared basil pesto

$^1/_4$ cup finely chopped, rinsed and drained, bottled roasted red peppers

20 oz. soft milk goat cheese, softened at room temperature (2 cups)

3 Tbs. bottled black olive tapenade

Drain pesto in a small fine-mesh sieve set over a bowl 15 minutes.

Line oiled loaf pan with a sheet of plastic wrap large enough to allow overhang on all 4 sides. (Parchment paper makes a smoother-looking torte.)

Blot peppers well between paper towels to remove excess liquid.

Spread about one fourth of cheese evenly over bottom of loaf pan and top with all of pesto, spreading evenly. Drop $^1/_2$ cup cheese by tablespoons over pesto and spread gently to cover. Top with chopped peppers, spreading evenly. Drop another $^1/_2$ cup cheese by tablespoons over peppers and spread gently to cover.

Spread olive tapenade evenly on top, then drop remaining cheese by tablespoons over olive paste spreading gently to cover. Cover the pan with another sheet of plastic wrap and chill at least 8 hours. Remove plastic wrap from top of pan and invert torte onto a serving plate, then peel off remaining plastic wrap. Let torte stand at room temperature 20 minutes before serving.

Serve with crackers or toasted French bread. Serves 8 – 10.

For a vivid description of what "under escort" meant, we have the funeral procession of JAMES TUNNAH who was born in Edinburgh, Scotland, and came to Little Rock as a stone cutter. He established the city's first marble works where he advertised: "All orders for Monuments, Head and Foot Stones of any kind or style will be promptly filled ... Parties wishing anything in this line will do well to call on me." He produced some of Mount Holly's most imposing monuments until his death in 1882 when he, too, was buried there. The *Arkansas Gazette* reported on October 10, 1882: "Religious services were held at his home. On their conclusion the coffin was removed to the hearse and the mournful cortege moved east on Markham to Center and up that street to the cemetery. The order of the procession was as follows: first was the consolidated brass band, toning forth the solemn strains of a march for the dead; then followed the Knights Templar in full uniform, and of which body the deceased had been an officer and an honored member; next came the hearse, followed by the members of the Western Star and Magnolia lodges of the Masonic order. A long line of carriages closed the procession. Ere the procession moved a large concourse of citizens had gathered in front of the residence and lined the sidewalk as far as Center Street. At the grave the solemn, beautiful, and expressive rites of the Masons were performed, and all that remained of James Tunnah was gently lowered into the bosom of Mother Earth."

In 1823 Little Rock attracted a young scholar from Massachusetts named JESSE BROWN, who established the town's first school. This coed elementary school expanded in 1826 and became the Little Rock Academy. Jesse placed an ad in the *Arkansas Gazette* stating that for only forty-four dollars a student could learn spelling, writing, arithmetic, reading, grammar, geography (with maps!), history, book-keeping, chronology, Italian, and French.

At the same time as the school was opening, an independent young woman named LOUISA CLARK left Vermont to teach in the Indian Territory. When she reached Little Rock she learned that there was trouble among the Indians and decided to teach at the new academy instead. For years the teacher and headmaster "courted," both becoming early members of the First Presbyterian Church in 1828.

In 1835 the devoutly religious Louisa decided to become a missionary to the Indians. As she was leaving town, Jesse finally proposed; and the couple were married in the spring of 1836. Jesse later served as both postmaster and mayor before his death in 1846. Louisa died in 1849. Both are buried at Mount Holly.

Toasted Chicken Rolls

18 slices raisin bread
3 Tbs. finely chopped green onion
Salt to taste
$1/8$ tsp. curry powder

2 cups finely chopped cooked chicken
$1/2$ cup mayonnaise
$1/4$ cup butter

Trim crusts from raisin bread slices. Roll bread slices lightly with rolling pin to flatten a bit. Combine chicken, onion, mayonnaise, and salt to taste. Spread filling over bread slices. Roll up each slice like jelly roll. Heat butter with curry powder until melted. Brush over rolls. Arrange rolls in shallow baking pan. Bake in very hot oven (475 F.) about 10 minutes until rich, golden brown. Serve hot.

Note: Untoasted rolls may be covered with foil and stored in refrigerator for later toasting if desired. (Kroger makes a raisin bread without cinnamon.)

Crab Filled Puffs

2 cups cooked crab meat

1 cup finely chopped celery

1/3 cup pickle relish

3 Tbs. lemon juice

1/4 cup chili sauce

1 cup rice (cooked in chicken broth)

2 Tbs. minced onions

2 hard cooked eggs (chopped)

1/4 cup mayonnaise

Mix above ingredients together and season with salt and pepper. Have 48 small cream puff shells ready to stuff and eat.

As Little Rock grew, it became apparent that a public burial ground was needed. On February 23, 1843, CHESTER AND MARY ASHLEY and their kinsmen, the Beebes, executed a deed for four blocks "for burial purposes" to the Town of Little Rock. These four square blocks became Mount Holly Cemetery, which has remained constant in size from the beginning. This act was just one of many benefits that Ashley, born in Amherst, Massachusetts in 1791, provided to the young state of Arkansas.

The Ashley home was known for its hospitality and was described as "a large and stately dwelling with lofty columns ... shaded by trees of the primeval forest. Adjoining was the flower garden under the care of Mrs. Ashley, who was extremely fond of flowers, and who was very successful in their cultivation; for years, flowers that bloomed in her garden went forth to crown many a bride and to deck many a bier." It was there that the Ashleys lived until the Federal troops occupied their home as headquarters during the Civil War. Mary Ashley survived the war by one month, dying in the house of relatives on May 25, 1865. She is buried at Mount Holly beside her husband, who died in Washington, D.C., in 1848 while serving as U.S. Senator from Arkansas.

In 1820, when Ashley came to the place where Little Rock later arose, it was simply a point where the road to Missouri crossed the Arkansas River, and was known as the "Missouri Crossing."

Deviled Eggs with Capers

6 hard-boiled eggs

1 Tbs. mayonnaise

1 tsp. garlic oil *

2 tsp. capers, chopped

1 Tbs. finely chopped fresh chives

1 tsp. Dijon mustard

1 tsp. red wine vinegar

Salt and freshly ground pepper to taste

Peel eggs and cut in half. Remove yolks to a small bowl. Use a wooden spoon to mash the yolks. Add the chives, mayonnaise, mustard, garlic oil, and vinegar to yolks and mix well. Stir in the capers and season to taste with salt and pepper.

Fill cavities of egg whites with the egg yolk mixture. Cover and refrigerate until ready to serve.

*You can make garlic oil by peeling and mashing three cloves of garlic and putting them in a sterilized pint jar. Fill the jar with olive or vegetable oil. Keep jar tightly sealed in a cool, dark place and it will last for months.

Born in New York in 1795, ROSWELL BEEBE took part in the War of 1812 as a musician. When he came to Little Rock he joined Chester Ashley in real estate. In 1843 they donated the four blocks of Mount Holly to the city of Little Rock to be used as a cemetery; and they both bought lots, even though they had given the cemetery to the city.

Beebe's main interest was railroads, and he was instrumental in getting tracks laid between Memphis and Little Rock. He also was one of the main organizers of the Cairo and Fulton Railroad and served as its first president.

He died in 1856 in New York and was buried in Greenwood Cemetery there and later moved to Mount Holly. He loved his railroad so much that he had the words Cairo and Fulton put on his tombstone.

The town of Beebe is named for him.

ANITA REASONER was a piano teacher, one of whose pupils was Chelsea Clinton. After one of her lessons, there were two stray kittens in Mrs. Reasoner's front yard; and the black one with white paws jumped right into Chelsea's arms. "Socks" became the first cat of Arkansas and followed Chelsea to Washington, becoming the first cat of the whole country. (Photo below.)

Socks and the President's retriever, Buddy, did not get along. The President compared their relationship to Northern Ireland or the Middle East. When the Clintons left the White House, Socks moved in with Betty Currie, the President's secretary, and enjoyed his semi-retirement until his late teens.

Socks died February 20, 2009. His ashes are at the Arkansas Governor's Mansion and in an urn at the Clinton Presidential Library. Little did Mrs. Reasoner know how far-reaching the encounter in her front yard in 1992 was to be.

Smoked Turkey Ball

1 cup ground smoked turkey   1 8-oz. pkg. cream cheese   3 Tbs. mayonnaise

Make turkey ball. Chill. Roll in 2 Tbs. chopped parsley and $1/2$ cup chopped pecans. This freezes well for later use.

FAY HEMPSTEAD was born in 1847 in Arkansas and married Gertrude O'Neale in Virginia in 1871. The couple returned to Arkansas where Gertrude was a charter member and president of The Aesthetic Club and her husband was a lawyer, an active Mason, and a pioneering Arkansas historian. He produced a three-volume *Historical Review of Arkansas*, among other publications.

When he was 84, Hempstead revealed one of his most charming reminiscences, writing about "The Blue Buildings in Little Rock" for the local newspaper. He recalled that blue was a popular exterior color for houses and business buildings in the early days of the city. All types of buildings were painted this color, whether they were frame, brick, or weather-boarded log houses; and since paint was expensive, the pioneers often used whitewash with indigo or bluing added. He remembered a number of the blue buildings that existed in Little Rock when he was a child. These included the first sanctuary of Christ Episcopal Church, the brick building on Main Street occupied by the firm of McLain and Badgett, the home of Judge Fields, the Garrett home, the Anthony House (hotel), the large brick City Hotel that stood on the bluff overlooking the Arkansas River, and rows of small shops that lined Markham Street.

STUFFED FRUITS

Prunes with Walnut Filling

2 oz. cream cheese, room temperature

12 pitted prunes

1 Tbs. chopped walnuts

Walnut halves to garnish

In a small bowl, beat cream cheese and walnuts until blended. Stuff mixture into prunes and garnish. Refrigerate before serving. Makes 12.

Figs with Camembert

¹/₂ lb. dried figs   3 Tbs. Port   1 4-oz. whole Camembert cheese

In a bowl, combine figs and Port. Cover and let soak several hours. Then cut a slit in each fig; gently hollow inside of fig with your finger. Cut cheese in as many pieces as you have figs; fill each fig with a piece of cheese. Makes about 15.

Fresh Dates with Ginger

¹/₂ lb. fresh or dried dates   4 oz. cream cheese, room temperature

1 Tbs. chopped crystallized ginger   1 tsp. grated lemon peel

Remove pits from dates. In a small bowl, beat cream cheese, ginger, and lemon peel until blended. Stuff mixture into dates. Makes about 15.

Dr. Vitus S. Barré Jr.'s Duck Pâté

Boil 2 whole mallard ducks (or the equivalent in duck breasts) with several stalks of celery and several diced onions until the meat separates easily from the bone. Debone the meat and set aside. In a food processor combine 1 onion, a clove of garlic, 1 Tbs. of curry powder, and the duck meat. Blend to a paste, adding equal parts of mustard and mayonnaise (about $^1/_2$ cup each). Add Tabasco and/or cayenne pepper to taste. Chill and serve with assorted crackers.

John T. Williams's Hot Minced Clam Canapes

4 oz. package cream cheese, softened
1 tsp. horseradish
Dash Tabasco
$^1/_2$ tsp. Worcestershire

1 tsp. lemon juice
Dash paprika
7 oz. can minced clams, drained and cleaned

Do this ahead if desired. Work cream cheese with fork until creamy. Add minced clams, lemon juice, horseradish, Worcestershire, paprika, and Tabasco. Refrigerate. About 15 minutes before serving, spread clam mixture on large fresh mushrooms. Arrange on baking sheet. Bake 300–325 degree oven about 15 minutes.

JOHN WILLIAMS was a founding partner of Mehaffy, Smith and Williams and was Chancellor of the Episcopal Diocese of Arkansas.

Corn Cakes with Tomato and Sour Cream / Yogurt Sauce

1 ½ cups frozen whole kernel corn (Use frozen corn in a package like a pound of sausage,
plus ¾ small can of corn, drained)

1 cup all purpose flour	½ cup cornmeal	1 ½ tsp. baking powder
½ tsp. salt	¼ tsp. baking soda	¾ cup milk
½ cup buttermilk	2 Tbs. butter, softened	⅛ cup sugar
1 egg, slightly beaten	Chives	Cherry tomatoes, quartered

Tomato and Sour Cream Sauce (see recipe)

Thaw frozen corn and pat dry with paper towels. Line a baking pan with foil, lightly grease the foil. Spread corn in prepared pan. Bake in a 450 degree oven for 10 minutes; stir. Bake about 10 minutes more until golden brown, stirring once or twice. Remove from oven, set aside. (You can sprinkle some smoked flavoring over the corn before cooking—stirred in.)

In a medium bowl, combine flour, cornmeal, baking powder, salt, and baking soda.

In a 2 cup glass measure, combine milk and buttermilk.

In a large mixing bowl, beat butter with an electric mixer on medium to high speed for 30 seconds. Add sugar and egg; beat until well combined. Alternately add flour mixture and milk mixture, beating on low speed after each addition—just until combined. Stir in corn.

Heat a lightly greased griddle or heavy skillet over medium heat until a few drops of water dance across the surface. For each pancake, spread about 2 Tbs. batter in a circle about 2" in diameter. (You can make larger ones and cut them in half after they are cooked and cooled.)

Cook over medium heat until pancakes are golden brown, turning to cook second side when pancake surfaces are bubbly and edges are slightly dry (about 2 or 3 minutes per side). Serve immediately or keep warm in a loosely covered ovenproof dish in a 330 degree oven. Serve with Tomato and Sour Cream Sauce. If you like, garnish with cherry tomatoes and chives. Makes 8 to 10 side dish servings.

(Pancakes may be cooked the day before and served at room temperature. Still good!)

Prep: 20 minutes for baking and about 15 minutes for mixing. Cook each batch 4 minutes.

Tomato and Sour Cream / Yogurt Sauce

In a medium bowl, combine:

$^1/_2$ cup dairy sour cream

$^1/_2$ cup coarsely chopped cherry tomatoes

2 Tbs. finely chopped onions

$^1/_4$ tsp. freshly ground black pepper

Hot sauce to taste

$^1/_2$ cup Greek yogurt

$^1/_4$ cup snipped fresh chives

$^1/_2$ tsp. salt

$^1/_4$ tsp. garlic powder

Makes about 2 cups

Family reunions are a southern tradition. All over Arkansas they take place, usually in the summer months, with family members gathering to eat, laugh, tell the same stories, argue the same topics, and simply enjoy being together. It is a wonderful way to celebrate the oldest members of the family and welcome the newest members. The Nixon family reunion, held the first Sunday in June each year, is typical. Family members from all over the state bring everything from buckets of Kentucky Fried Chicken (contributed by the non-cooks) to delicious homemade desserts (from the true cooks) and even innovative new recipes. This recipe falls in that last category and is good as is—or with just the sauce prepared to serve over cold shrimp, avocado, etc.

Pickled Tuna

4 cans (5 oz.) solid white
 water packed tuna, drained

1 jar capers with juice

$^1/_2$ to $^3/_4$ cup sour cream

1 small red onion, sliced paper thin

1 large lemon, washed good and sliced thin

3 Tbs. wine vinegar

Break tuna into large pieces and mix with onions and lemon rings. Add capers, caper juice, vinegar, and sour cream. Toss lightly and refrigerate. This may be prepared a couple of days in advance. It needs to be refrigerated at least overnight. Serve with party rye.

Chutney Roll

1 (8 oz.) package cream cheese

1/2 cup chopped (sliced) almonds, toasted

1/2 tsp. dry mustard

1/2 cup Chutney, finely chopped

1 Tbs. curry powder

1/2 cup finely chopped
unsalted dry-roasted peanuts

Combine first 5 ingredients in mixing bowl, stir well, shape into a log. Wrap in wax paper and chill one hour. (Mixture will be soft.) Roll log in peanuts. Chill several hours or over-night.

Serve with assorted crackers.

Yield: 1 6-inch roll

Potted Stilton with Port Wine Reduction

1 stick butter

1 1/3 cup Stilton cheese
(two 150 gram wedges)

Cut the Stilton cheese into small cubes and mix it gently with soft butter until you obtain a nice creamy cheese mousse that is ready to be served.

In a pan mix together 1 3/4 cup Port Wine and 1/2 cup sugar. Bring it to a boil and reduce by 50%. (about 20 min.)

Let it cool, and it is ready to serve on Stilton cheese mousse.

Serve in small ramekins with torn French or sour dough bread. Very rich, but good.

Jane Brett's Cheese Ball

2 packages (8 oz.) Philadelphia cream cheese

¹⁄₂ jar of some very sharp cheese (small jar)

1 small onion, minced

1 cup minced parsley

¹⁄₄ lb. Roquefort cheese

1 large Tbs. Worcestershire sauce

1 cup minced pecans

Salt and red pepper to taste
    (use red pepper abundantly)

Cream all the cheese together and work with spoon or hand to assure an even, creamy mixture. Add the onion, the Worcestershire sauce, salt and red pepper, but only half of the nuts and parsley. Mix thoroughly and roll into a ball.

Spread the other half of the nuts and parsley (mixed) on a board and arrange evenly, then roll the cheese ball in it. Place in a covered dish in the refrigerator until ready for use. Will keep for several days and is better the second day. Serve on a large platter surrounded by crisp crackers.

Jezebel Sauce

1 18 oz. jar pineapple preserves   1 18 oz. jar apple jelly

1 small can dry mustard   1 small jar of horseradish

1 Tbs. cracked pepper

Mix all together, blending well.

Put in jelly jars and refrigerate. Will keep indefinitely, but must be refrigerated. This recipe makes several small jars of sauce. Good on cream cheese, ham, etc.

Jezebel will last a long time and is best if made at least a day or two before use. If you are in need of something similar in a hurry, the following will work:

1 cup peach preserves   1 Tbs. prepared horseradish

2 8 oz. packages cream cheese, softened.

Mix preserves and horseradish. Mix cream cheese and $^1/_4$ cup of preserve mixture together. Form into a ball and pat down the center (indent top). Spoon the rest of the horseradish mixture over the top and down the sides of the ball. Serve with crackers.

Curried Olives

In a blender, combine 1 Tbs. instant minced onions and 2 Tbs. lemon juice and allow to stand for 5 minutes. Add 1 Tbs. curry powder, blend, and gradually add $^1/_2$ cup salad oil. Pour mixture over 1 $^1/_2$ cups drained stuffed green olives in a jar. Cover and refrigerate for at least 3 days to mellow flavor. Drain before serving.

LILLIAN SCOTT (Mrs. Conoway Scott) made "Lillian's Orange Pecans" during the depression and sold them locally as well as in New York City. Following the devastating flood of 1927, the Great Depression almost destroyed the plantations outside of Little Rock. Elmhurst Plantation at Scott had 800 acres of land in danger of being lost. At that time cotton was the main crop of the plantation, and pecans were a secondary crop that was taken care of by the "women folk." As the depression deepened, Lillian Scott, whose husband owned Elmhurst, urged the farm workers to gather the pecans for her; and in her kitchen she began making a confection that had always been one of her family's favorites—orange candy pecans. Her cousin, Samuel Reyburn, was at that time president of Lord & Taylor Department Store in New York. He agreed to market her candy; and with the pieces arranged 24 to a box on lace doilies, in elegant white satin boxes, "Lillian's Orange Pecans" were soon sold not only in Lord & Taylor, but at retailers throughout the United States. Lillian's pecans got the Scotts through the long time of trial.

Lillian's Orange Pecans

Boil 1 1/2 cups of sugar and 1/2 cup of orange juice until thermometer reaches 234 F, or a small quantity of the mixture dropped in cold water forms a soft ball.

Take off stove and add grated rind of small orange and 3 cups of pecan halves. Stir until mixture looks cloudy.

When it begins to sugar, drop each pecan to a marble top.

Lillian's granddaughter, Debbie Scott, is making these today and selling them in certain outlets. She was kind enough to share this recipe with us.

A scene from "Tales of the Crypt"

Lagniappe

❧ RECEIPTS ☙

Kathy Worthen shared with us these interesting pre-Civil War documents that were called "receipts." The use of "recipes" came much later. These are from a very old Receipt Book of Clementine R. Watson, Kathy's great, great grandmother.

To make washing Fluid
To one galon of soft soap such
as is made by the usual
method of boiling the lye of
wood ashes and fat together
take four ounces of salsoda half
a galon of rain or soft water
and half a gill of spirits of tur-
pentine Place them all in a pot
over a fire and allow the mixture
to boil a few minutes It is then
ready for use and can be kept in
an earthen or stone ware
vessel In using this Fluid the
clothes intended to be washed
should be soaked in water 10
or 12 hours say over night an
then to a ten or twelve galon boiler
full of clothes covered with water add
one pint of fluid boil briskly 15 minu
and then rinse them out in fresh
water it will not mutch rub

Clementine R Watson
for Book for Receipt

to dye Black
take a sufecient quantity
of water to even your thread
and blue stone to turn the
water a light green put in
your thread and simmer it
slowly fifteen minutes wring
out your thread get cleane
water put in your Logwood
and stir it until dissolved
put in your thread boil as
before fifteen minutes

Eb dye walnut dye with the
leaves or bark in the light men
with the root in the dark

A Taste of Ireland

Some of the oldest graves in the cemetery are those of the Irish who proudly remembered their homeland on their tombstones. Many were Irish artisans who arrived in the early 1830s to work on the construction of the Old State House, bringing their families with them. On their gravestones we see RICHARD MURPHY, born in County Dublin in 1788; FRANCIS MCCANN, born in Ireland in 1792, fought in the War of 1812; PATRICK CUDDIHY, born in 1814 in Tipperary, Ireland; his wife MARGARET, born in Cork; and his brother WILLIAM, born in Ireland in 1820; ANNA CAVANAUGH, born in Ireland in 1812; and SARA CECELIA KINNEAR (whose husband JAMES was a "cordwainer"), born in Ireland in 1827. In honor of all the Irish lads and lasses buried at Mount Holly we present a "recipe" from an "Irish Cookery" book for an

Oatmeal Face Pack:

Mix one egg with enough oatmeal to make a stiff paste. Pat onto face and leave for 15 minutes. Rinse off with warm water. This gently cleanses sensitive skin.

It works!

ALVIN FONES BUTTERFIELD was known for her beautiful and very special floral arrangements. When the depression began she turned this into a business by starting The Remembrance Flower Shop with the help of her husband ROBERT, who had been until that time employed in a building and loan company.

Tussie—Mussies

During the Colonial days, Americans called a tight twist of flowers Tussie-Mussies or Colonial bouquets instead of nosegays. These Tussie-Mussies were bouquets made up of flowers and scented herbs and carried by ladies for fashion as well as necessity. In early times these fragrant bouquets were held at the nose to filter the smells of the period and were used by both men and women to combat the stench from the deplorable sanitation of the streets.

Most holders were made by local artisans and were trumpet shaped since these bouquets were hand-held rather than pinned to the clothing. The First World War was the end of the era for carrying Tussie-Mussies.

The Victorians often used the language of flowers to express their sentiments. Specific herbs and flowers were used in bouquets to convey messages. Today some brides carry these bouquets for their weddings and have the flowers used reflect the sentiments indicated in the language of flowers. A rose is always a good choice for the center. Roses indicate many ideas by their various colors. A red rose means beloved, love or I am worthy of you. Rosemary stands for love, remembrance, fidelity, and wisdom and may be included in the bride's bouquet as well as worn by groomsmen.

Some other flowers and herbs and what they stand for: Daisies—innocence, patience, and a token of affection; Violet—humility; Lily of the Valley—purity; Lily—symbol of the virgin birth; purple Statis—gratitude; Fern—sincerity; Sage—wisdom; Mint—virtue and cheerfulness; Scented geranium leaves— comfort and gentility; Ivy—friendship; Rue—clear vision and virtue; and Thyme—bravery, courage, and strength.

Soups

Many of Little Rock's citizens were born or treated at TRINITY HOSPITAL, established in 1924 by Dr. Mahlon Ogden and four other doctors. In 1931 the doctors began a pre-payment medical plan that raised a storm of controversy in the medical community but appealed to over 5,000 contract patients, including 2,000 individuals and 100 groups (businesses and other organizations). There was a monthly charge of $2.50 per person, and each office visit cost fifty cents. A charming practice of this hospital was the addition of a little poem and a flower on each food tray, with perhaps a bowl of early day "penicillin"—also known as chicken soup.

Chicken soup is best if made with homemade chicken stock. A leftover chicken carcass with bits of meat on the bones (even a pre-cooked chicken from the grocery store) makes good stock when broken up, simmered with chunks of carrots, onions, celery, a tied up bunch of thyme or parsley, salted with a chicken bouillon cube, and strained. If you really want something divine—add two chicken feet, although for this you may need to raise your own chickens!

Chicken Soup

1 Tbs. butter	1 finely chopped onion
1/4 cup flour	4 1/2 cups chicken stock
Salt & pepper to taste	1 cup sliced cooked chicken
Bouquet garni	Finely chopped parsley

Melt butter and fry onion lightly without burning; add in flour and mix well together. Gradually add stock, bring to boil and season to taste.

Add diced chicken and bouquet garni, bring back to boil, cover and simmer for 20 minutes.

"DR." JOHN W. BEIDELMAN was a pharmacist, not a doctor; but he was generally called Doctor. His real interest was music and his family paid for his musical education with the promise that he would never use his talent for pay. He and his wife were a happy couple, but they did not agree on religion. She was a staunch Presbyterian and he was an equally staunch Episcopalian. For many years he played the organ at First Presbyterian Church and was active at Trinity Cathedral as vestryman and delegate to conventions. He would undoubtedly have volunteered his services to his own church had it not been for the fact that the Bishop's daughter was also an accomplished organist.

Dr. Beidelman was public spirited and was instrumental in forming the Little Rock Athletic Association—usually referred to as the Boathouse—and was president for 13 years. The annual regattas were highlights of the social season for over 50 years.

Black Bean Soup

1 pint dry black beans	3 qts. water
1/4 lb. salt pork	1/2 pound stewing beef
1 carrot, sliced	2 onions, chopped
1 Tbs. salt	3 cloves
1/8 tsp. mace	1/4 tsp. cayenne
3 hard-boiled eggs, sliced	1 lemon, thinly sliced and seeded
1/2 cup sherry	

Soak the beans overnight in 1 qt. of the water. The next morning, pour the water and beans into a large soup kettle and add 2 qts. water, salt pork, beef, carrot, onions, salt, and spices. Cover and simmer for 3 to 4 hours. Remove the meat and put the soup through a sieve, or blend in a blender until smooth. Serve piping hot in a tureen garnished with hard-boiled eggs and lemon slices. Add the sherry just before serving. Serves 20.

Philadelphia Pepper Pot

(Traditionally thought to have been invented for George Washington and his troops during the winter at Valley Forge.) Serves 8

1 lb. cleaned tripe $1/2$" cubed	1 lb. veal shank in 2 pieces
4 to 6 whole black peppercorns	1 tsp. salt
4 Tbs. butter	1 cup onion, chopped
$1/2$ cup celery, chopped	$1/2$ cup green pepper, chopped
3 Tbs. flour	2 potatoes diced $1/4$"
Dried hot red pepper, crushed	Fresh ground black pepper

Cover veal in water (2"). Bring to boil over high heat. Add peppercorns and salt, reduce heat, simmer partially covered for 2 hours until tender. Remove meat from bone; cut in $1/2$" pieces. Strain liquid and reserve 6 cups. In same pot sauté onions, celery, and green pepper in butter 5 minutes until soft. Add flour and mix well. Return 6 cups of liquid slowly until soup thickens. Add potatoes and meat. Simmer 1 hour. Correct seasonings. Add enough dried red pepper and black pepper to give unique peppery taste.

(We suggest trying this without the tripe.)

When WILLIAM CUMMINS died on April 7, 1843, his family faced a dilemma. A city ordinance had been adopted in March prohibiting interments at any burying ground other than Mount Holly after May 1. A deed had been executed to designate the land for the cemetery, but none of the lots were to be sold until a public sale in May. His family wanted William buried at Mount Holly right away—and so he was. The lot where he was buried actually was not purchased until 11 years later when his brother Ebenezer bought three lots, designating one as William's.

William Cummins was not only the first person buried at Mount Holly, but also had one of the most well-documented funerals. The April 8, 1843, record book of his Masonic lodge states that: "The Masons assembled and formed a procession which proceeded from the lodge to Markham street, up Markham to Cumberland to the residence of our deceased brother, William Cummins, and from thence to the Methodist church where an appropriate prayer was delivered by Brother Stevenson and then proceeded to Mount Holly cemetery where the remains were deposited in solemn form."

Bean Soup

$1/2$ pound uncooked navy beans

1 cup diced potatoes

Salt & pepper

1 Tbs. parsley

$3/4$ pound ham shank (or salt pork)

3 large tomatoes,
    skinned and finely chopped

$3/4$ cup diced onion

Soak beans overnight. Rinse, cover with fresh water. Simmer beans until tender and drain. Cover ham with cold water and simmer until tender, skimming off fat. Add potatoes, onions, and beans to the ham. Simmer. Close to end of cooking, add tomatoes and spices.

Lentil Soup

1 box lentils (Any color. The red ones are the ones Esau sold his birthright for.)

Pick over and rinse the lentils, cover with stock or broth (water for vegetarians) and cook slowly for 30 minutes. In a separate pan cook 2 diced onions in 3 Tbs. olive oil until they become transparent. Add to lentils. Add 4 carrots and 4 stalks celery, diced, and 3 minced garlic cloves. Add 1 tsp. ground cumin and simmer it all about 30 minutes. Salt and pepper to taste. Check often. If it is too dry, add a little water; if too liquid, cook longer, uncovered. When ready to serve add either 1 Tbs. vinegar or 1 Tbs. dry wine to the pot. Garnish with parsley or sour cream if desired. (Add sliced cooked sausage for a main dish.)

This is better the next day and freezes well, too.

Catfish Soup

¼ lb. bacon or salt pork	2 large onions, chopped
2 carrots, chopped	1 Tbs. parsley
1 stalk celery, chopped	2 lbs. catfish cut in large chunks

Fry bacon until crisp. Remove and save. Add onions, celery, and carrots and cook until soft. Add fish, parsley, salt and pepper, and just enough water to cover. Simmer until fish is tender but firm. Mix 3 eggs, 1 Tbs. flour and 1 cup of milk. Heat and add to soup along with the bacon. Heat until thickened. Serve hot.

Sometimes an epitaph is a mystery. This is true of the monument to MARCUS ELDER, who was a caretaker of the farm north of the river owned by WILLIAM WOODRUFF, JR. On Sunday morning, October 24, 1886, Major Woodruff visited the farm at Big Rock and found the body of Marcus "Maro" Elder lying face down on the floor. Near a broken window was a chair where Maro had been sitting. His gold watch was still in his vest pocket, and there was no indication that someone else had been there. It was assumed that the window shattered when the caretaker fell from his chair, dying of natural causes at least a week earlier.

Because of the condition of the body, a coffin was sent for immediately and placed on a ferry to cross the river to Little Rock. Marcus was buried that very day at Mount Holly in the lot of his uncle, JAMES A. HENRY. The next day Capt. Henry visited Maro's house and discovered a bullet on the floor opposite the broken window. He took "the bullet that did the fatal work" to the sheriff and it was determined that "the victim was foully murdered." The body was exhumed and a post-mortem clearly showed the path taken by the bullet. "Steps were taken to apprehend the assassin." (All quotes from the *Arkansas Gazette*.)

The sheriff sent two deputies with an arrest warrant to the home of a neighbor suspected of the murder. The suspect's home was surrounded by a rock wall with small holes where he could shoot out but was protected inside. The deputies "made a reconnaissance of the fortifications, and after a council of war decided that it could only be captured by strategy. They procured a couple of axes and returned to the house. Calling the occupant to the gate, they informed him that they were a couple of woodchoppers who desired the use of his grindstone to sharpen their axes. The neighbor agreed to accommodate them, for which favor a small consideration was promised." When he came out to take them to the grindstone they seized him, overpowered him after a struggle, hand-cuffed him, and headed for the jail. A grand jury found a true bill against the man, who on his way to jail kept repeating: "If I did kill him, it can't be proved on me; and it's nobody's business if I did kill him." And that is the story behind Marcus Elder's epitaph, which says simply: "Killed at Big Rock."

DR. ISAAC FOLSOM was a doctor in Lonoke who was instrumental in starting the medical school and the first public clinic in Little Rock. He and Mrs. Folsom had no children, but he loved them and equipped his office with a pet monkey, a trick dog and a parrot to entertain his young patients. When he died in 1892, he left $20,000 to the medical school with the provision that his name appear on all the diplomas. This amount doesn't sound like much now, but it was a fortune in the early 1890s; and his wish was granted. His name still appears on the diplomas.

Folsom died in September, 1892, in Lonoke and is buried in his private mausoleum, made of "buttered brick." During prohibition, the mausoleum was used as a drop-off for bootleg whiskey.

Winter Squash Soup

3 large onions, chopped	1 cup celery, chopped
1 clove garlic	4 Tbs. butter
3 cups chicken stock	2 cups cooked squash, mashed
2 Tbs. parsley, chopped	1 tsp. each fresh rosemary and savory
2 cups heavy cream	($1/2$ tsp. dried)
Salt and pepper to taste	Nutmeg

Saute onions, celery, and garlic until golden in 2 Tbs. of the butter. Add in chicken stock with cooked squash, rosemary, savory, and parsley. Bring to a boil; then simmer for 10 minutes. Add 2 Tbs. butter. Remove from heat and add cream. Season with salt and pepper. Dust with nutmeg and serve in a warmed tureen. Serves 8.

Cajun Gumbo

Served at the Hanger House Mardi Gras Ball

4 (14 oz.) cans chicken broth   7 or 8 oz. boxed Gumbo mix with rice

5 or 6 chicken breasts or 2 large cans prepared chicken breast, drained

1 lb. Polish sausage, sliced thin. (Broil sausage for a few minutes and drain fat.)

1 package (10 to 14 oz.) frozen okra   1 green pepper, chopped

1 red pepper, chopped   1 onion, chopped

Add a good handful of Cajun Seasoning

Add about 1 tsp. of black pepper   2 (14 oz. bags) frozen salad shrimp

Combine all ingredients except shrimp. Bring to boil and simmer for 25 minutes. Add frozen shrimp and simmer another 5 minutes.

Serve with warm French bread, of course!

FREDERICK and FRANCES HANGER hosted a Mardi Gras Ball in their home at 1010 Scott each year. This is their original Gumbo recipe, modified. It's easy and very tasty.

A Toast

Typical of the toasts heard at Little Rock dinner parties in the early 20th century was this one by FRANCES MARION HANGER.

"Here's a toast to the guest of honor

Who is making her debut—

May she have so many suitors

That she won't know what to do!"

Borsht

1 cup of broth (chicken if you plan to serve hot, beef stock if served cold)

2 cans of beets with liquid

2 Tbs. sour cream

2 tsp. lemon juice

$\frac{1}{2}$ tsp. salt

$\frac{1}{4}$ tsp. pepper

Thin yellow peel of 1 lemon

Put all ingredients in blender for 2 minutes or until well blended. Chill, or heat for serving hot. Put a heaping teaspoon of sour cream on top of each serving. Garnish with chives or small bits of raw spinach. Recipe, which makes 1 $\frac{1}{2}$ pints and serves 6, may be doubled.

PEG SMITH'S *Borsht is good to serve in mugs in the living room, with an extra mug of breadsticks to pass. Peg got this recipe from Bea Cochran and said, "There must be as many versions of this as there are various spellings of 'borsh,' 'borsch,' 'borsht'... this version must be strictly American. On a trip to Russia we had borsht often, but it usually was a thick hearty soup with much meat and shredded cabbage, and, of course, the ubiquitous potatoes."*

Gazpacho

Soak 1 loaf bread—squeeze dry. (Try Challah bread.) Peel 2 lbs. tomatoes & 5 cucumbers. Add 1 cup olive oil, $\frac{2}{3}$ cup good vinegar, 2 to 4 cloves garlic, 1 tsp. lemon juice, $\frac{1}{3}$ an onion, $\frac{1}{3}$ a green pepper, $\frac{1}{2}$ tsp. salt, pepper and basil. Mix in blender.

Chill thoroughly. Serves 12.

Cucumber Soup

2 cucumbers, roughly chopped

1 Tbs. finely chopped fresh dill

$^1/_8$ tsp. white pepper, or to taste

4 cups buttermilk

1 Tbs. finely chopped fresh parsley

Place all ingredients in $^1/_2$ gallon jar. Screw lid on firmly and blend by shaking vigorously. Refrigerate until well chilled. Shake or stir well before serving. Cool and refreshing!

ZEB WARD was born January 14, 1822, in Cynthiana, Kentucky, and married MARY WORTHEN in 1851. He was in the Mexican War and the Gold Rush, was a Mississippi steamboat clerk, was lessee in both the Kentucky and Tennessee State Penitentiaries, and fought in the Civil War on the Union side. A contractor, he built the first Little Rock Water Works system in 1877. He was president of the Little Rock and Mississippi Railroad and the builder-owner of Little Rock Oil Mills and Cotton Compress. All the brick structures on the block of Markham to 2nd and Ringo to Cross Streets he had built with convict labor. Zeb fed the legislature Thanksgiving dinner in 1871 and showed them other favors from time to time. Someone remarked at the time, "If he don't feed his convicts any better than he ought to, he at least knows how to entertain his friends."

Michael Dougan wrote in *The Arkansas Odyssey* that Ward was an unsavory character who held the lease on the state penitentiary and supposedly had a fortune of half a million dollars, most of it from dealings with the state.

In 1880 President Grant came to Little Rock to patch up friction caused by the Brooks-Baxter War. Peg Newton Smith remembered her family's story about the ladies on 9th Street putting chairs on their front lawns for Grant's presidential parade, and turning the backs to the street. When he got to the Capital Hotel, he stood for hours greeting well-wishers and became very weary. Someone suggested that Zeb Ward could replace him, as they looked a lot alike, and give the president a rest, which Ward did. The plan worked for a while until an ex-con shouted to the world that he would know Ward anywhere. Zeb Ward died December 28, 1894.

Laura Nichols's Cold Curried Cream Cheese Soup

2 cans concentrated beef consommé–do not add water.

12 oz. cream cheese $^1/_2$ clove garlic

Salt & pepper & curry powder to taste (consommé is salty)
Blend, then chill.

GOOD WITH: *Cheese Spread for Sandwiches*

$^1/_2$ cup butter, 1 cup cream cheese, $^1/_2$ cup grated parmesan (seasoned to taste with paprika, curry, and Nature's Seasoning). Spread on English muffin. For hearty appetite, add sliced ham and tomato, add a dollop to the top and bake until warm. Broil 1 minute to brown top cheese.

Cold Tomato Soup

1 can tomato soup   1 cup light cream

Season with grated onion, Worcestershire, Tabasco, and the juice of 1 lime. Add very finely chopped celery. Serve with toasted slivered almonds. MARGARET CAMPBELL

Santa Fe Soup

2 lbs. ground beef
2 small packs Ranch
    Salad Dressing Mix
1 can Tomatoes (wedges)

1 large onion
1 can Black beans
1 can Pinto beans

2 packages Taco Mix
1 can Kidney beans
2 cans White Corn

Cook ground beef and onion together and drain off grease. Add all other ingredients including all the fluids in the cans. Simmer for 2 hours. When serving, garnish with condiments: shredded Monterey Jack cheese, chopped green onions, and sour cream.

This is easy and good to fix and freeze to pull out on a cold day.

Salads & Condiments

ABSALOM FOWLER was born in Kentucky and was a staunch Whig. He attended the 1836 Constitutional Convention, was secretary of the Legislative Council, and was elected to the Arkansas House of Representatives. He and William Woodruff exchanged insults regularly. Fowler was an attorney and must have been successful to have built his large house that was finished in 1840. He drew up the plans for a home that was planned for entertaining; but apparently they never had any company.

MRS. FOWLER (ELVIRA BOSWELL) came from an un-churched family but became interested in the Presbyterian Church and talked to the minister, the Rev. James Wilson Moore, about joining. He was skeptical, telling her that his church was very strict and "did not tolerate many things that were acceptable in other churches." She insisted, and turned her life over to the church; and afterwards "she evinced no desire for the amusements of the world." She died in 1842.

Piquant Avocado Salad

1 clove minced garlic	1 tsp. salt
1/2 tsp. fresh pepper	1/2 tsp. sugar
1/2 cup olive oil	3 Tbs. wine vinegar
3 avocados, sliced thin	1/4 cup finely chopped green onions
1 Tbs. minced parsley	2 Tbs. chopped capers

Beat all seasonings in salad bowl. Add avocados, scallions, parsley, and capers and toss until well coated. Chill 1 hour. Serves four.

DANIEL RINGO was Chief Justice of the Arkansas Supreme Court and U.S. District Judge before the Civil War. Although he was 61 years old when the Civil War began, he was a Confederate soldier. It is unlikely that this prominent attorney knew of his kinsman, "Johnny Ringo," who was at the same time on the other side of the law. Johnny, one of the most feared gunfighters in the west, was shot in Tombstone, Arizona, in 1882. Daniel was buried in 1873 beside his wife and young son at Mount Holly.

Yellow Squash Salad

10 squash, sliced

3 Tbs. vinegar

3 Tbs. olive oil

Basil and/or oregano

Cook squash in salted, boiling water for 3 to 5 minutes just until barely tender. Drain. While hot, add other ingredients. Chill. Add pepper and salt if desired. Add chopped chives and parsley. Serve cold, garnished with parsley. (Serves 6 to 8.)

MR. AND MRS. HALEY BENNETT (Julia, but called "Scrap" by her friends) had a big celebration to dedicate the cornerstone at their new home, Stonegate. They were carrying on a tradition started by Scrap's grandfather, JUDGE ELBERT H. ENGLISH, Chief Justice of the Arkansas Supreme Court, when he built his house between 8th and 9th on Center Street in 1859.

Stonegate's dedication was a solemn affair with speeches, prayers, and a poem written by ROBERT M. BUTTERFIELD, designated permanent poet laureate of the house. Below is the first stanza of one of Butterfield's poems:

> "There's a quiet sylvan neighborhood beyond the city's din,
>
> Whose pastoral seclusion is devoid of noise and strife;
>
> Where ugliness is left without and loveliness within,
>
> And mockingbirds sing all around, and peaceful beauty rife."

The Bennetts continued this anniversary party annually with all of the fanfare for many years.

"Aunt Scrap" Bennett's Salad

1 pkg. lemon gelatin	$1/2$ cup boiling water
$1 1/4$ cups ginger ale	$1/8$ tsp. salt
4 Tbs. chopped nuts	4 Tbs. finely cut celery
1 Tbs. finely chopped crystallized ginger	1 cup assorted fruits, diced (pineapple, cherries, and peaches)

Dissolve gelatin in boiling water and add ginger ale. Cool until slightly thickened, fold in nuts and fruits. Chill in greased mold until firm.

(You can eliminate the water and use all ginger ale instead.)

Cold Vegetable Salad

1 can seasoned green beans

1 large can tiny peas

1 small bottle pimento

2 carrots, thinly sliced

Salt and pepper to taste

1 can Chinese vegetables (LaChoy)

1 can water chestnuts

$1\,^1/_2$ cups chopped celery

1 onion (large), thinly sliced

Drain well. Place all ingredients in large dish. Mix marinade of $^3/_4$ cup vinegar and 1 cup of sugar. Pour marinade over vegetables and refrigerate until well chilled.

THE ARKANSAS TRAVELLER

SCENE IN THE BACK WOODS OF ARKANSAS.

TRAVELLER,— TO SQUATTER.— CAN YOU GIVE ME SOME REFRESHMENTS AND A NIGHTS LODGING?— SQUATTER NO SIR?—HAVEN'T GOT ANY ROOM, NOTHIN TO EAT (FIDDLES AWAY)—TRAVELLER... WHERE DOES THIS ROAD GO TO?—SQUATTER,— IT DONT GO ANYWHERE, IT STAYS HERE,— (STILL FIDDLING)— TRAVELLER.— WHY DONT YOU PLAY THE REST OF THAT TUNE? SQUATTER—DONT KNOW IT.— TRAVELLER.—HERE GIVE ME THE FIDDLE— PLAYS.

"The Arkansas Traveller"

Print

1870

Made by Nathaniel Carrier & James Ives

From the permanent collection of the Historic Arkansas Museum

CEPHAS WASHBURN was a young minister from Yale Divinity School who brought his family in a wagon through ice, water, and quicksand to become missionaries to the Indians of Arkansas. They reached the two-building settlement that today is Little Rock on the 4th of July, 1818; and Washburn preached to 14 men in a log cabin. He later stated that this was the first sermon ever preached in Little Rock; and it was perhaps the longest—lasting two hours.

Cephas established Dwight Mission School for the Cherokees near present day Russellville and continued missionary work there and in Oklahoma until 1840. Afterwards, as an evangelist, he traveled throughout Arkansas. On his way to Helena to deliver a series of sermons, he died in 1860. He was buried at Mount Holly, where his son EDWARD PAYSON WASHBURN was buried beside him nine days later.

Edward Payson Washburn was a portrait artist who supplemented his income by painting scenes of the Arkansas frontier. His most famous work, painted in 1855, was the "Arkansas Traveler." The public love of genre painting and an increasing interest in the new southwest caused Currier & Ives prints of the "Traveler" to be sold nationwide.

This painting was based on a true story that involved several residents of Mount Holly: U.S. Senator Ambrose Sevier, U.S. Senator Chester Ashley, Territorial Governor William Fulton, and well-known planter Sanford Faulkner. During the election of 1840, these men were on a campaign tour of western Arkansas with their candidate for governor, Archibald Yell. When they became lost in the Boston Mountains, Col. Faulkner approached a squatter's cabin to ask for directions, and a frustrating but hilarious dialogue took place. Faulkner later related the story at Yell's inaugural ball (and at other events); and it became famous in song and painting. It begins with the traveler being bested at every question by an old man sitting in front of his cabin playing the same part of a tune over and over. The squatter declares there is no food, nothing to drink, and only a leaky-roofed spot in the cabin where the strangers could sleep. Finally, the frustrated traveler asks him why he doesn't play the rest of his tune. The indifferent fiddler says there isn't any more, but the visitor takes the fiddle and plays the complete tune. (At this point, Sanford Faulkner would pick up his fiddle and play "The Arkansas Traveler.") The amazed squatter had never known the last of the song and shouted to his wife: "Sal, stir yourself round like a six-horse team in a mud hole." He orders food, whiskey, knives to eat with, and to the traveler he says: "Play away, stranger, yew kin sleep on the dry spot tonight."

Edward Payson Washburn was born in 1831 at the Dwight Mission established for the Indians, and died in Little Rock in 1860. A granite marker honoring this young artist was placed on his grave in 1958 with a few bars from "The Arkansas Traveler" as his epitaph.

When ARTHUR CAMPBELL of Scott was going to the State Fair in Little Rock, his wife, MARGARET, asked him to take a pound of butter and enter it in the fair. Most people at Scott had a cow and therefore lots of butter. When he went to the office they told him that they did not have such a category, but he noticed a lot of blue ribbons and offered the butter to the lady in exchange for a blue ribbon. She accepted. He never told his wife what took place, and Margaret thought until her dying day that she had won it.

When the Campbells' son Don was little, he said he wanted to leave home. His mother, Margaret, said she would help him pack and he set forth with his little knapsack. He wasn't gone long (probably watched all the way) and when he returned he remarked, "Same old dog?"

Margaret Campbell's Marinated Chicken Salad

2 whole fryer chickens

1 can large sliced mushrooms

1 small/medium jar pimento-stuffed olives

1 large can whole artichoke hearts, drained and cut in half

1 avocado

1 bell pepper, sliced

1 large white onion, sliced thin

DRESSING:

$^1/_4$ cup olive oil

$^1/_2$ cup vinegar

$^1/_2$ tsp. pepper

$1^1/_4$ cup (or less) Wesson oil

1 tsp. salt

Steam (or boil) chickens. When done, chill, de-bone, and cut in large pieces. Slice bell pepper. Slice onions very thin. Cut stuffed olives in half. Marinate for several hours in dressing. Marinate avocado separately, to put on top of each serving. Serve on bed of bib lettuce with strips of avocado across the top. Makes 10 large servings.

Served with half of a big tomato, a cup of fresh fruit and hot rolls, with Angel Food cake and ice cream, this makes a full meal.

DR. PHILO OLIVER HOOPER was born in 1833 into an early Arkansas family, attended Nashville University in Tennessee, and graduated from Jefferson College of Medicine in Philadelphia in 1856. He married GEORGIE CARROLL of Alabama in 1859. He served in the Confederate Army, then settled in Little Rock as a physician with particular interest in mental health. A Mason, an Odd Fellow, and a trustee of Arkansas Female College, Dr. Hooper helped organize the Medical Department of Arkansas Industrial University—now the University of Arkansas—serving as faculty member and first dean in 1879.

He was elected president of the American Medical Association in 1883, but he is mostly remembered for starting the Insane Asylum (Arkansas State Hospital) and serving as its superintendent for many years. The legislature had delayed erection of an appropriate building for mental patients for several years because of bickering over the site and the Brooks-Baxter War in 1874. Governor Churchill was finally able to get a bill passed, at Dr. Hooper's prodding; and the building was finished in 1882. It was called Arkansas Lunatic Asylum; and it has been overcrowded ever since, even with the various additions that have been made over the years. Happily, the name was at last changed to Arkansas State Hospital. The Little Rock street between UAMS and the State Hospital is named for him: Hooper Drive.

Spiced Peach Salad

1 package lemon Jello
1 large jar pickled peaches, drained
  (Save juice.)

1 package orange Jello
1 can mandarin oranges, drained
  (Save juice.)

Use peach and orange juice with enough water to make $2\frac{1}{4}$ cups. Boil and pour over Jello and dissolve. Cool. Blend peaches until pureed. When Jello is partially set, add fruit and congeal.

Good with ham.

DR. FRANK VINSONHALER was born in 1864 in Missouri. He was a Belgian Consul for Arkansas and Dean of the University of Arkansas Medical School (1927-1939). He was instrumental in building the "new" Medical School facility in 1939 across from MacArthur Park. (It had been located in the Old State House.)

As a member of the XV Club he was host one evening in the early part of the 20th century. During the formal dinner, the butler whispered something in the doctor's ear and the doctor excused himself. After an interval he returned to the dining room with the news that the cow had entered the back porch and had gotten stuck in the turn of the back stairs. The kitchen help and the good doctor had not been able to budge her, so everybody got up (obligatory black tie and all) and were eventually able to get her unstuck and the proper dinner continued. (Several townspeople kept cows in their back yards at night and had them taken out to pasture, which was not far away in those days, during the day.)

MRS. VINSONHALER, nee WRENETTA BEIDELMAN, was born in 1871 and was married to the doctor in 1898. She was a kind, gentle person. After a well-known cad and bounder died, the family went around the dining room table relating terrible things about the poor man; but when it came her turn she said, "He had beautiful handwriting."

Arctic Freeze

2 packages cream cheese (3 oz.)

2 Tbs. sugar

1 cup crushed pineapple

2 Tbs. mayonnaise

1 1 lb. can whole cranberry sauce

$^1\!/_2$ cup pecans (broken)

1 cup whipped cream

Soften cheese, blend in mayo and sugar. Add fruit and nuts. Fold in whipped cream. Pour into an 8 $^1\!/_2$ x 4 $^1\!/_2$ x 3 $^1\!/_2$ pan. Freeze firm, 6 hours or overnight. To serve, let stand at room temperature about 15 minutes. Serve on lettuce. 8 to 10 servings.

Marion Vinsonhaler McCain

JOHN PARKS ALMAND was a prominent architect until his death in 1969. Among his many major projects were Little Rock Central High School, Memorial Hospital in North Little Rock, the old City Hospital, First Presbyterian Church, the old Asbury Methodist Church, and Oak Forest Methodist Church. His wife, FRANCES REEVE EDMONDSON ALMAND, was a leader of women's suffrage and temperance movements in Arkansas and was president of Medical Arts Realty Co. in Hot Springs.

Frances Almand's Asparagus Salad

1 can asparagus soup	8 oz. sour cream
1 pkg. gelatin	2 Tbs. lemon juice
$^1/_2$ cup water	Salt, Tabasco & pepper to taste

Soften gelatin in water, then heat until dissolved. Add rest of ingredients. When it begins to thicken add cut up asparagus and/or other seasonings such as capers, olives, herbs, celery, etc. Place in greased mold.

Little Rock Central High School

Molded Summer Salad

Press softened cream cheese around a pecan half. Slit cherry and insert pecan/cheese. Prepare black cherry Jello according to directions. Put 2 to 3 stuffed cherries in individual molds and pour Jello over. Jell until firm. Amounts of cherries, Jello, etc. depends on how many molds you wish to make.

Orange Fruit Salad

2 cups mandarin oranges, well drained	2 packages (3 oz.) orange gelatin
1 small can crushed pineapple	$^1/_2$ cup chopped pecans

Mix gelatin as directed on box, except substitute the can of crushed pineapple for one cup of the cold water. Add oranges and nuts and chill thoroughly. Serve cut into squares and top with whipped cream or mayo.

Wrenetta Worthen Williamson

NICHOLAS PEAY was born in 1784 in Virginia. The name was originally LaPeay, pronounced Pay. The family moved to Kentucky, where he married JULIET NEILLE. Peay fought in the War of 1812 and in one of the Indian wars, where he became a warm friend of General Harrison at Tippecanoe. After the war, he invested most of his assets in a good friend's business. The "friend" went east on a trip and never returned. Peay lost everything. To avoid embarrassment he and his family left Kentucky and came to Little Rock in 1825, bringing all their belongings on flatboats down the Mississippi River.

There were only nine families in Little Rock at the time, but he saw the need for a hotel and started one on Markham Street between Main and Scott Streets. As Little Rock grew, he replaced his small hotel with a larger building. Peay retired to a plantation "near the river, opposite the little Maumelle Springs" and died there May 3, 1843. His was the second burial in Mount Holly.

Bess Peay Pipkin's Millionaire Salad

2 whole eggs	5 Tbs. lemon juice
2 Tbs. butter	1/2 lb. cut marshmallows
1/2 cup blanched almonds	1 #2 can diced pineapple
1 #2 can white cherries	1 cup cream, whipped

Beat eggs, add lemon juice, butter, and marshmallows.

Cook in double boiler until marshmallows dissolve. Fold in almonds and fruit. Cool. Fold in 1 cup whipped cream. Freeze overnight in mold or pan of your choice. Serve frozen, but not too hard.

Modern marshmallows came into use in 1850.

ROBERT D. LOWRY was born in Omaha, but his family moved to Little Rock when he was small. He graduated from the Wharton School, then served with the Navy in World War II. His business was insurance, and he served on several civic boards including the transition of Little Rock Junior College to the University of Arkansas at Little Rock. He was an active worker for integration in the public schools.

He married BETTY SUE CUNNINGHAM, a direct descendant of D. Matthew Cunningham, Little Rock's first mayor. She was a long-time member of the Mount Holly board and served a term as president.

(The Cunninghams spent their vacation at the popular Mount Nebo in the 1930s. As they were going home down the steep road, their son Jiggs said "Mom, I ..." And she said, "We can't talk now." Then he said, "But Mom ... Bet ..." She said, "I told you not to talk now; you can tell me when we reach the bottom." He gave up and they finally got to level ground. She said, "Now, what is it you wanted to say?" He replied, "Betty Sue is still up at the Lodge.")

Bing Cherry Mold

1 large can bing cherries
1 small pkg. lemon Jello

$^1/_2$ cup sugar, or to taste

Bring juice from cherries to a boil, add sugar and Jello and cool.

When it begins to thicken, add $^3/_4$ cup chopped nuts and the cherries.

For salad, serve with Feta or Blue cheese sauce. For dessert, use whipped cream. The Sam Peck Hotel used small ring molds and filled the center with chicken salad.

This was a favorite of Betty Sue Lowry's when entertaining.

GEORGE A. WORTHEN was born in 1816 in Kentucky. He married ELIZABETH McMILLIN in 1846; after she died he married LOUISA BOOKER. He was a merchant and a planter when he came to Little Rock. Worthen was a competitive gardener, especially with tomatoes, which were a novelty in the early 1800s. People at first were afraid to eat tomatoes, as they are members of the deadly nightshade family. Then when they did not seem dangerous, people decided that not only were they good, but they were good-for-you.

Worthen died in 1864; but there was no obituary for him, as the *Arkansas Gazette* was not published during the Civil War between September 12, 1863 and May 5, 1865, because they could not get the paper to print it on.

(From the *Arkansas Gazette*, 30 July, 1852)

LARGE TOMATOES
LITTLE ROCK NOT BEAT YET

We noticed, a few weeks ago, a fine tomato weighing 17 $^1/_2$ oz. which had been presented to us by our friend, Mr. George A. Worthen, of this city. On seeing which, our friend, Mr. William Van Valkenburg, of Warren, Bradley county, wrote us that he had weighed three fine tomatoes, grown in his garden, two of which weighed 1 $^3/_4$ lbs. each and the other 1 $^1/_2$ lbs.–and triumphantly exclaims, "Now best that, George!" These we must confess were very fine ones, and hard to beat–but our friend Van must yield the palm of victory to his friend George, who a few mornings after presenting us with the first, showed us one that actually weighed 38 oz. (or 2 lbs. 6 oz.). If our friend Van, or anybody else in Arkansas, or elsewhere, can beat this, we would like to hear of it, and to receive a few of the seeds of the premium tomato.

Herbed Tomatoes and Cucumbers

Slice tomatoes several hours before serving and sprinkle with salt and chopped fresh basil. Wash cucumbers with soap and water. Do not peel. Score with strong fork tines and marinate several hours with salt, white vinegar, and water in refrigerator. To serve, arrange tomatoes on platter around sliced cucumbers.

Curried Shrimp Salad

CURRIED MAYONNAISE:

1 cup mayonnaise

1/2 – 1 tsp. curry powder

1 tsp. honey

1/4 tsp. ginger

1 crushed clove garlic

1 Tbs. lime juice

SALAD:

1 lb. shrimp, cooked and chopped

1 apple, chopped (Granny Smith)

1 cup celery, chopped

Mix with mayonnaise and put in 1/2 avocado.

Top with teaspoon of chutney and sliced or slivered almonds

Rosemary Dyke says this is the best!

DR. MAHLON D. OGDEN, SR. was born in 1881. He was a lifelong resident of Little Rock, graduated from the University of Arkansas Medical School and taught surgery there. He married Sue Worthen in 1907. He was a Mason and served in World War I. His greatest achievement was to found Trinity Hospital, incorporated in 1923 and built in 1924. This pioneer effort in pre-paid medical care began in 1931, and his title was president of Group Health Foundation. There was so much opposition to this plan by other doctors that the group resigned from the American Medical Association rather than be kicked out. It thrived for several years, and in 1947 the group asked to be reinstated in the AMA. They were turned down. They tried again in 1948 and were accepted. Medicare would have duplicated Trinity's program. Unfortunately, Dr. Ogden did not live to enjoy his final acceptance; he was just ahead of his time.

SUE WORTHEN OGDEN (MRS. M. D. OGDEN, SR.) was active in the community. She was an organizer of the Parent Teacher Association, instrumental in establishing the Girl Scout movement in Little Rock, served on the national board of the Girl Scouts, helped to organize the Little Rock Community Chest, and was on the board of Mount Holly when the Community Mausoleum was built.

Bread & Butter Pickles, 25 pints

5 gallons cucumbers
($^1/_2$ bushel=large grocery bag)

25 cups sugar

2 $^1/_2$ tsp. ground cloves

5 tsp. celery seeds

30 small onions

2 $^1/_2$ cups non-iodized salt

7 $^1/_2$ tsp. turmeric

10 Tbs. mustard seeds

2 gallons cider vinegar

Bread & Butter Pickles, 5 pints

1 gallon cucumbers

$^1/_2$ cup non-iodized salt

1 $^1/_2$ tsp. turmeric

2 Tbs. mustard seeds

5 cups cider vinegar

8 small white onions

5 cups sugar

$^1/_2$ tsp. ground cloves

1 tsp. celery seeds

Wash but do not pare cucumbers. Slice crosswise in paper-thin slices. Slice onions thin. Mix salt with vegetables and bury pieces of cracked ice in the mixture. Cover with weighted lid and let stand 3 hours. Make syrup: mix sugar, turmeric, and cloves. Add mustard seed, celery seed, and vinegar. Cook until mixture reaches boiling point. Pour over sliced pickles. Place all over low heat and paddle occasionally with wooden spoon. Heat mixture until scalding hot, but do not boil. Pour into sterilized jars and seal.

Sunday suppers were lively family affairs around the Ogdens' dining room table, which easily accommodated twelve. These bread & butter pickles are legendary in the family of Sue Worthen Ogden. The family continues the canning tradition today, insuring they always have a good supply on hand.

As a transplanted Ohio native, ELEANOR TODD PATTY embraced her new Arkansas home and its possibilities from the moment of her 1946 arrival. She married a fifth generation Arkansan, CLAIBOURNE WATKINS PATTY, SR., in 1933. He introduced her to the beautiful Ouachita area with its lakes. Their beloved weekend retreat on Lake Hamilton continues as a family vacation site. There her chutney might appear at a Thanksgiving dinner and her cornmeal pancakes on a summer morning to "lay down a good base" for her grandsons before their day of water activities.

Colonial Apple Chutney

2 lbs. tart apples (about 5 medium)	1 lemon with peel, seeded and chopped
1 1/2 cups granulated sugar	1/4 cup firmly packed dark brown sugar
1 cup seedless raisins	1 Tbs. chopped candied ginger
2 cloves garlic, crushed	1 1/2 tsp. salt
1/2 tsp. crushed red pepper	1/4 tsp. cinnamon
1 cup cider vinegar	1/3 cup rum (or applejack)

Peel and core apples; chop finely. Combine lemon, sugars, ginger, garlic, salt, spices, and vinegar in a large saucepan. Bring to boil and cook rapidly 5 minutes, stirring constantly. Add apples and raisins, reduce heat, simmer uncovered, about 20 minutes, until mixture is thick and syrupy, stirring occasionally. Remove from heat and stir in rum or applejack. Fill hot, sterilized jars and seal. Process 15 minutes in hot water bath. Makes about 5 half-pint jars.

GEORGIA LINCOLN SHIPTON (Mrs. James Ancil Shipton) lived in the Egyptian house on South Broadway. In the early 1930s, summers were especially hot. One year there were thirty consecutive days over 100 degrees, and there was no air conditioning. People were on their own to cope. Mrs. Shipton, when at home, wore a minimum of clothing and sat in front of a wash tub filled with a large piece of ice with an electric fan behind it. It worked quite well.

Her husband, BRIG. GENERAL JAMES ANCIL SHIPTON, had a distinguished military career: U.S Military Academy, Spanish-American War, organizer of the Anti-Aircraft Service of World War I, Military Attache to Brazil, and officer of the French Legion of Honor. He also belonged to several clubs in New York, San Francisco, and Washington and to the XV Club in Little Rock.

At that time many people made salads with mayonnaisee, but they were beginning to make their own "French dressing" to use in tossed salads.

French Dressing

1 cup olive oil

2 Tbs. grated onion

$^1/_2$ cup sugar

1 Tbs. paprika

$^1/_3$ cup vinegar

   (or a combination of vinegar and lemon juice)

$^1/_2$ cup ketchup

Salt and pepper to taste

Basic Vinaigrette

1 $^1/_2$ tsp. Dijon style mustard

Pinch salt

$^1/_4$ cup extra virgin olive oil

2 Tbs. red wine vinegar

Fresh ground black pepper

You can substitute Balsamic vinegar and add cut-up basil if desired.

Alice Campbell's Sweet Tomato Relish

1 market basket* of ripe tomatoes, peeled and chopped

3 pints of vinegar

2 cups sugar

1 dozen large green peppers, seeded and chopped

1 dozen large onions, peeled and chopped

2 large kitchen spoons of salt

2 tsp. each of powdered cinnamon, cloves, and allspice.

Bring ingredients to a boil, then turn down to simmer for about 2 hours. Requires a very large pot to cook, and as a processing pot. Leave the top ajar, or off for the last hour or the mix is too watery. Process for 5-10 minutes in a boiling water bath. Makes 21 pints. A medium large Dutch oven will hold ½ recipe.

*Trial and error decided that 1 market basket of ripe tomatoes equals 1 peck or 16 pounds. A large kitchen spoon in her era, equals ¼ cup; so 2 spoons equals ½ cup. Alice Campbell's granddaughter, Robin Orsi, says that this relish is to die for on purple-hulled peas, especially when they are fresh, and on black-eyed peas for New Year's Day.

WILLIAM MOORE CLARK was born in 1921 in Monroe, Louisiana; and ELIZABETH HALL CLARK was born in 1920 in Nashville, Tennessee. He donated his legal services to Mount Holly for many years, and she was a board member. Typical of their inspired retorts to awkward questions was this. A friend asked Billy Moore how much acreage his mother had left him and he replied, "Not nearly enough."

Billy Moore Clark's "The World's Best Mayo"

Beating for 10 to 15 seconds after each addition of oil is the secret that makes this mayo stay firm and good for a long time.

2 egg yolks	2 Tbs. apple cider vinegar
1 tsp. salt	2 cups oil
2 Tbs. lemon juice	1 tsp. black pepper

Put egg yolks, vinegar, and salt in bowl. Beat with mixer for about 2 minutes, until a slight, hardly noticeable thickening occurs. Add $^1/_4$ cup of oil with a spoon a few drops at a time over a period of about 3 minutes. Allow 5 to 10 seconds of beating between each addition of oil so that thorough mixing occurs. Add remaining 1 $^3/_4$ cups of oil a Tbs. at a time, allowing 10 to 15 seconds of beating between each Tbs. When mayo is thick, add lemon juice and pepper. Leave the mixer on for about 1 minute after the juice has been added. If the mayo is too thin, add a little more oil slowly. Taste it and add more salt, vinegar, and lemon juice if you want. Makes about 2 cups.

ADOLPHINE FLETCHER TERRY (MRS. DAVID DICKSON TERRY) was born in 1882 and was one of the first Arkansans to attend an eastern college, Vassar. When she returned, she settled down to improving her native town. Her first accomplishment was to organize the first juvenile court in Arkansas. After that she had a part in almost every improvement that took place. She was instrumental in founding the Little Rock Public Library and was one of its early users and a long time trustee. The Terrys, like several other families, kept a cow; and when the regular milker couldn't be there, Adolphine went to the library, found a book that explained how to milk a cow, and proceeded to do so.

She was a leader in the Head Start program, helped organize the Orchestra (although she was not a great music lover, she saw the need for live music), and supported the beginning of the Arts Museum, now known as the Arkansas Arts Center. When Governor Faubus closed the high schools, she called up Arkansas Gazette editor Harry Ashmore and said, "The men have failed again; I'll have to call the women." And she did. The Women's Emergency Committee to Open Our Schools was started in her parlor under the watchful eye in the painting of her father in his Confederate uniform. This faithful group of women worked all year and got the schools back open. Both Harry Ashmore, who received a Pulitzer for his newspaper coverage, and Adolphine Terry stressed obeying the law of the land. The Terry Library is named for her.

After attending an affair at the new Arts Museum where a "visiting fireman" said a few words, and then a lot more, and there were no chairs, she said that she had reached the age that she was going to give up something every year and next year she was going to give up "swelling the crowd."

Terry Mansion

Ham Baste

2 Tbs. minced parsley   2 cloves minced garlic   1 tsp. thyme

1 tsp. marjoram   2 tsp. ground cloves   2 Tbs. dry mustard

6 Tbs. brown sugar   2 Tbs. honey (or molasses)   2 bay leaves

Mix all with red wine vinegar to moisten

Sherry for basting

Cook ham in foil. Last 30 minutes fold back foil, trim rind, and slash fat. Apply baste.

Lime Horseradish Condiment

1 cup hot water   1 pkg. lime gelatin

1 jar horseradish   1 cup sour cream

Dissolve gelatin in hot water, add other ingredients, whip to mix, pour into square Pyrex dish, chill until firm. Cut in squares to serve.

(Great with baked ham. Robin Orsi)

DAVID DICKSON TERRY was born in 1881. He was an attorney, rendered service in World War I, represented Little Rock in the Legislature and Arkansas in Congress for four terms. He was instrumental in bringing Camp Robinson to Little Rock and Pine Bluff Arsenal to the state. He was a member of the XV Club, the Boathouse—where he was an outstanding athlete—and after his retirement he spent the rest of his life working as a volunteer for flood control—an urgent need after the devastating flood of 1927. The lock and dam below Little Rock is named for him.

MARY FLETCHER TERRY was born in 1914 with a calcium deficiency and never walked. She got around with a specially made tricycle and graduated from Mount Holyoke College, earned a Master's degree in social work from the University of Chicago and worked for many years at Children's Hospital. Her crowning achievement was to travel to Africa alone, with two cur dogs, to visit her aunt, Charlie May Simon Fletcher, who was staying at Dr. Albert Schweitzer's compound. No American airline would take two pets, but the Dutch airline KLM agreed to take them both. She returned home with the dogs and two African parrots and had her great sense of humor through it all. One of her parrots only knew the whistle that sailors made when a pretty girl walked by. This parrot (when it wasn't perched on Mary's shoulder) would sit in the trees of the Terry home and whistle at everyone who passed by. She loved animals and was organizer and charter member of the Pulaski County Humane Society. Her several dogs were from the street.

Once when a cousin had had a recipe printed in the paper, Mary sent her a post card saying that her mother was proud of her cousin, since nobody had ever before asked to print her mother's recipe for store-bought ham and canned pineapple.

Cranberry Relish

1 lb. fresh cranberries	1 navel orange
1 firm apple or pear (or both)	1/2 cup dates, pitted
3/4 cup sugar or more if desired	

Pick over cranberries after washing. Coarsely chop in food processor with quartered orange (unpeeled), quartered and cored apple, and/or pear (unpeeled), dates, and sugar. Add broken pecans before serving.

Keeps well in refrigerator. Great with turkey and dressing.

Marshmallows

1 envelope reliable gelatin

1 cup fine granulated sugar

1 tsp. vanilla

1 $^{1}/_{4}$ cups cold water

Few grains of salt

Soak gelatin in $^{1}/_{2}$ the water for 5 minutes. Put remaining water and sugar in saucepan and boil without stirring until syrup will spin a thread when dropped from the spoon. Remove syrup from the fire, add soaked gelatin and let stand until partially cooled; add salt, flavoring and cool until mixture becomes white and thick. Pour into pans thickly dusted with powdered sugar (having mixture 1 inch thick). When thoroughly congealed, turn out on a board, cut in cubes and roll in powdered sugar. This recipe makes about 100 marshmallows.

This recipe is from the Woodruff Family Cookbook 19th/20th century. Several words were illegible because it was handwritten so we put in what we thought it might have said. The collection is at the Historic Arkansas Museum.

Herb Butter

1 cup butter, softened

1 Tbs. chopped fresh parsley

$^{1}/_{2}$ tsp dried whole basil

1 Tbs. chopped chives

$^{1}/_{2}$ tsp. dried whole marjoram

1 tsp. lemon juice

Combine all ingredients, and beat until light and fluffy. Store mixture in a covered container in refrigerator until ready to use. Yield: 1 cup.

In costume for "Tales of the Crypt"

Bread

Hot Cross Buns
(Traditional for Good Friday)

1 cup scalded milk	3 cups flour	$1/2$ cup sugar
3 Tbs. butter	$1/4$ cup warm water	2 eggs
$1/2$ tsp. cinnamon	$1/2$ cup currants	$1/4$ cup lemon or orange peel
Touch of cloves	Powdered sugar	Milk
Yeast		

Combine warm milk, sugar, butter, and salt. When room temperature, add yeast and one egg and mix well. Sift and add flour, cinnamon, and cloves. Add currants and citron. Mix thoroughly. Cover and let rise until double in size. Shape into round buns and place close together in a well-greased pan. Let rise again. Beat an egg, and brush each bun. Cut a cross into each bun. Bake in hot oven for 20 minutes. Brush crosses with sugar moistened with milk.

JAMES PHILIP EAGLE, besides being a governor of Arkansas (1889-1893), was a former officer in the Confederate Army; a large landholder; and an ordained Baptist minister, serving as president of the Baptist State Convention for 24 years. Politics seemed to have become so corrupt that it was decided that a man of the cloth would bring some trust to the office of governor. When he was 44 years old he married MARY KAVANAUGH OLDHAM (Mamie to her family and friends) and moved her to Arkansas in 1882. When Eagle was elected Governor in 1888, he and Mamie purchased the old Crittenden home at 219 East Seventh in Little Rock. Mamie made their home one of the most charming and hospitable in the state. During the time her husband served as governor, the receptions at their home were the events of the year. They never had any children but had many nieces and nephews.

In a tribute to his wife, Governor Eagle said, "She was self-renouncing in her fidelity to what she conceived to be right, self-denying and self-sacrificing in her devotion to the cause she espoused, gentle as the evening breeze, pure as the snowflake, tender as the smile of the rose, firm as the granite hills."

Margaret Campbell's Yeast Rolls

1 ¼ cups lukewarm milk

3 eggs

⅓ cup sugar

4 ½ cups sifted flour

2 packages yeast

2 tsp. salt

⅓ cup melted butter

Beat eggs and add sugar, salt, and melted butter until smooth. Then add yeast/milk combination, stirring well, until smooth. Then add sifted flour.

Put in greased bowl and let rise to top. Knead on board, taking up as little flour as necessary (do ½ or ⅓ of the dough at a time). Roll out thin. Cut with cutter and dip roll in melted butter (real butter), then fold over. Put in greased pan. Let them rise till double in bulk. Bake in 350 degree oven until not quite brown. Cool and put in baggies to freeze.

Martha Wheeler Campbell's Corn Muffins

1 package cornbread mix, such as Jiffy

1 large can whole kernel corn, drained

6 oz. sour cream.

1 large can (14 ¾ oz.) creamed corn

2 eggs

1 stick butter, melted
  in 8" x 8" pan you are going to bake in

If you wish, add salt, pepper, and/or optional herbs such as oregano, dill or cumin to taste.

Mix all of the above together and pour into pan or muffin tins. If using muffin tins, spray with vegetable spray. Bake at 350 degrees for 35 – 40 minutes until slightly brown on top.

This will be a Corn Spoon Bread consistency. If you prefer a firmer muffin, add another package of cornbread mix.

Virginia Spoon Bread

1 cup cornmeal	2 cups boiling water
1 Tbs. butter	1 tsp. salt
1 tsp. sugar	2 eggs well-beaten
1 tsp. baking powder	1 1/4 cups milk

Pour boiling water over cornmeal, beating all the time to prevent lumping. Add butter, salt, and sugar. Cool. Add to eggs, baking powder, and milk. Bake 425 degrees for 45 minutes.

DR. PHILLIP BURTON was born in Virginia and died in Little Rock on September 14, 1875, at the age of 80. He came early and lived to be very old and eccentric. A lady patient asked him if he could do something to make quinine taste better. He replied, "No, madam; if all hell was a sugar house, it would not sweeten one drop." To another lady who had been in Little Rock only a short time, when told she had malaria and wanted to know what to do about it, he replied, "We give calomel, quinine and sanger." She said she knew what calomel and quinine were, but what was sanger? Sanger was his brother-in-law, the local undertaker. One time a friend persuaded the doctor to attend a service at Christ Episcopal Church to hear the Rev. R. B. Lee, who was very popular. When asked how he liked it, he said, "Not at all. All I saw was a damn blue streak going down the aisle." The federal soldiers whom he detested were the blue streak.

Rumor has it that he had 26 children, with three wives. This has not been verified, but the 1870 census showed that he had a three-year-old child and a young wife.

Corn Meal Puffs

Pour 1 cup boiling water over one cup of white corn meal to which $^1/_4$ tsp. salt has been added. Beat well and let stand for ten minutes. Then fold in stiffly beaten whites of 3 eggs. Drop from a spoon onto a buttered cookie pan and bake 20 minutes in a quick oven (425 degrees). Serves 4 to 6.

ELBERT H. ENGLISH was born in Alabama and moved to Little Rock in 1844. Always a strict Methodist, he considered becoming a college professor, then doctor; and finally he decided on law. He was admitted to the bar in 1839 and married JULIA AGNES FISHER in 1840. (Julia was president of the Soldiers State Aid Society during the Civil War.) Elbert practiced law in Little Rock and in 1854 he was elected Chief Justice of the Supreme Court. After Julia's death, he married Mrs. Susan A. Halsson Wheless. It was said he was "lifted from the bench after the war by the sword of Reconstruction." He resumed his law practice until 1874, when he was re-elected Chief Justice; and he continued until his death. He was Grand Master, Masonic Grand Lodge of Arkansas; a founder and secretary of St. John's College Board;* trustee of Arkansas Female College;** and prominent in the organization of the First Methodist Church. He died September 1, 1884, at Asheville, North Carolina.

*St. John's College was started in 1859, closed during the war, reopened and then permanently closed in 1879.

**The required uniform for young ladies, in the winter of 1858, was "dark, plain worsted dresses, with sleeves closed at the wrist, collars of plain linen, black aprons and sun bonnets, no superfluous article of dress will be allowed, and jewelry strictly forbidden."

Mrs. English's Hunter's Bread

1 1/4 cups flour	1/2 tsp. salt
3/4 cup cornmeal	1 cup milk
4 Tbs. sugar	1 egg
4 Tbs. baking powder	1 lb. bacon (this is correct)

Sift dry ingredients together. Beat the egg and combine with milk, beat into the dry ingredients thoroughly. Spread into a lightly greased biscuit pan, or 9" square pan or large loaf pan. Cut the bacon in small pieces and sprinkle over the top of the dough. Bake in 350 degree oven for 20 minutes. Serve with ducks or other game.

JOHN NETHERLAND HEISKELL led the *Arkansas Gazette* as president and editor from 1902 until 1970 when he became Chairman of the Board. Under his leadership it became, from a struggling obscure country newspaper, one of the most honored newspapers in the U.S. In 1958, the *Gazette* became the first newspaper in history to win two Pulitzer Prizes in the same year.

MRS. J. N. HEISKELL (Wilhelmina Mann) married when she was 19 and he 37. She founded the Little Rock Garden Club with a group of women she invited to her home in November, 1923.

MRS. FRED HEISKELL (Georgia) was a member of one of Arkansas's pioneer families. She was a daughter of WILLIAM ASHLEY and JOSIE CLENDENIN ROYSTON. Her paternal grandfather was a delegate to the first Constitutional Convention in 1836 and was president of the 1874 Constitutional Convention that framed the present state constitution. Her maternal grandmother's family, Isaac and Maria Watkins, were the principal founders of the city's first church in 1824. Mrs. Watkins's second husband, Rev. William Stevenson, switched the church's denomination in 1832 from Baptist to Christian; and it exists today as the First Christian Church. Mrs. Heiskell was the oldest member of the First Presbyterian Church and second oldest member of The Aesthetic Club. She also served on the Mount Holly Board.

Peabody Muffins

$3/4$ cup sugar	1 stick butter, softened	3 eggs, separated
$1/4$ cup milk	1 tsp. vanilla	1 cup flour, sifted
$1/2$ tsp. lemon juice	1 tsp. baking powder	$1/4$ tsp. salt

Cream butter and sugar. Add beaten egg yolks, milk, vanilla, and lemon juice. Resift dry ingredients and add. Fold in stiffly beaten egg whites. Don't over stir. Bake in greased muffin tins (about $1/3$ full) at 375 degrees for 15 – 20 minutes.

This is a family recipe that is a real favorite. Fred Harrison makes them at Christmas for his grandchildren when they spend the night. Ideally they are made in a tin for very small muffins. They make a delicious little bite!

DR. HENRY GEORGE HOLLENBERG was a key player in making penicillin a mainstream medicine during World War II and was an expert in amputations. He received the Legion of Merit Award. Actor Gordon Mills portrayed him in 1955 in a segment of CBS's television program "You Are There," recounting the rise of penicillin. Dr. Hollenberg was a well-known, very talented artist. He had the longest tenure, over 40 years, of any member of the XV Club. He held the honored position of scribe and delighted the men with his acerbic note-taking and one-liners. His meeting notes were famous for their humor.

Sappy's Biscuits

This quantity made 11 biscuits using a 2 3/4 inch biscuit cutter.

2 cups all-purpose flour	1/2 tsp. salt
1/2 tsp. baking soda	1/2 tsp. cream of tartar
4 tsp. baking powder (adjusting from 3)	2 tsp. sugar (adjusting from 3)
2/3 cup buttermilk	1/2 cup Crisco

Add all dry ingredients in mixing bowl. Stir to blend.

"Cut in" the Crisco. (Helps to cut the cold Crisco stick first with 2 knives into small pieces.) Add buttermilk and stir only enough to absorb all dry material into ball of dough. Lightly flour cutting surface. Cut dough in half, work by hand to a thickness of 1/2 inch. Use drinking glass to cut individual biscuits. Reshape dough and repeat. Add remaining dough to second half original ball and repeat. Last biscuit shaped by hand. Avoid excessive handling of dough to reduce toughness.

Preheat oven to 450 degrees. Cook for 10-12 minutes (check for desired color; add minutes to increase darkness) on non-greased cookie sheet. Remove to cool surface.

DAISY ANDREWS KEATTS was a trained nurse who was engaged to look after Mrs. James Keatts, Sr. When Mrs. Keatts died, her son JAMES KEATTS married Daisy. During the depression, Mr. Keatts lost his job; so Daisy started a catering business. At first, it was out of her house; then she became head of the Peacock Tea Room and later she took on the Tea Room on the mezzanine at Blass Department Store. People from all over Arkansas met there for lunch on Saturdays to enjoy Daisy's delicious creations.

Daisy Keatts's English Scones

2 cups flour	4 tsp. baking powder
1/2 tsp. salt	2 tsp. sugar
1/4 cup butter	1/2 cup milk

Mix and sift flour, baking powder, salt, and sugar. Cut in butter. Add beaten egg. Save 1 Tbs. milk and 1 tsp. egg to brush top. Roll out into shapes. Bake. Serve hot for luncheon or tea.

Daisy Keatts's Ginger Cheese Muffins

2 cups flour	3 tsp. baking powder
1/4 tsp. soda	1/2 tsp. ginger
1/2 cup molasses	1/2 tsp. salt
2/3 cup grated cheese	1 egg
1/2 cup milk	4 Tbs. cooking oil

Combine ingredients. Fill muffin tins 2/3 full and sprinkle with ginger and sugar. Bake 20 minutes at 350 degrees. For luncheon, serve with a fruit plate.

GEORGE ROSE SMITH was born in 1911 and PEG NEWTON SMITH was born in 1915. He became a lawyer and joined the firm his grandfather, U.M. Rose, started—one of the oldest law firms west of the Mississippi. After a few years he was elected Associate Justice of the Arkansas Supreme Court and remained on the bench for 38 years, the longest serving appellate court judge in the nation. He was a strict grammarian and his opinions were so well written that they were widely known and respected. He also liked to work and create crossword puzzles, several for the *New York Times*, and he was a member of The Boathouse.

Peg was interested in preservation and helped to save many historic structures. She was a founder of the Quapaw Quarter Association and on the board of Historic Arkansas Museum for 62 years and on the Mount Holly Board for nearly 50 years. She started the tours and picnics at the cemetery. She was president of the Little Rock Junior League and the Aesthetic Club.

The Smiths' usual dinner was 10 o'clock p.m.; and when they had company, it was even later. Every year they had a Fourth of July picnic at which they always served hamburgers. If the 4th came on a Friday, the Roman Catholics could not eat the meat; but not to worry, the hamburgers that George cooked on the outdoor grill were usually not ready until midnight, so by then it was Saturday. Their good friends learned to eat before they came.

Judge Smith once painted the Mount Holly bell house with a friend that he had recruited. They would work on it all day Saturday—while listening to Razorback games on the radio.

Carmelite Nuns' Whole Wheat Bread is from Laurie Smith Fisher and she says she makes it frequently. She was fascinated going with her father, Judge George Rose Smith, to buy bread from the nuns, before he started making bread himself. They got it through a small window in a door and spoke only to one nun in a darkened room, since the nuns had taken a vow of silence.

Judge Smith's Cracked Wheat Bread

1 cup milk, scalded

1 $^1/_2$ Tbs. molasses

6 to 7 cups flour

1 $^1/_4$ cups water

$^1/_2$ tsp. salt

1 package active dry yeast

1 cup cracked wheat cereal

(may be purchased in health stores)

Add water to milk, then yeast and other ingredients. Mix together with a kitchen spoon with enough flour for a smooth dough. Knead for 6 to 8 minutes for thorough mixing. Stretch dough, let rise in mixing bowl until double its size and punch down. You may let rise a second time and punch down, but it's not necessary. Spread in greased loaf pan and let rise to double its size. Bake in pre-heated 350 degree oven for 40 to 50 minutes.

Judge Smith had an amusing wrapper in which he distributed some of his gift loaves—"The Judge hands down a well-baked opinion."

Carmelite Nuns' Whole Wheat Bread

Sprinkle 3 packages of yeast in 4 cups warm water, stir, and let stand for several minutes. Then add 4 tsp. salt, $^1/_4$ cup of vegetable oil and $^1/_2$ cup (or more) of molasses. Then stir in flour—3 to 4 cups of white flour and 5 to 6 cups of whole wheat. (They used all whole wheat, but the white flour makes the dough rise more easily; and the bread is not as heavy.) Knead dough for about 10 minutes, until it has a good consistency. Put in greased bowl and flip over to grease the top. Let rise until double. Then punch down dough, and put in greased bread pans. Let rise until almost double.

Bake at 375 degrees 35 to 40 minutes, or until done. Cool on racks.

(We suggest using 1 cup molasses and also recommend cutting the recipe in half as it makes a lot and is heavy to handle.)

Banana—Nut Bread

½ cup Wesson oil	1 cup sugar
2 eggs	2 cups all-purpose flour
1 tsp. baking soda	3 crushed bananas
1 cup chopped pecans	

Cream oil and sugar; add beaten eggs. Add flour and soda alternately with crushed banana. Stir in nuts to which has been added 1 Tbs. flour. Pour mixture into greased 8" x 4" x 3" pan. Bake 1 to 1 ½ hours at 325 degrees. Check doneness by inserting toothpick into center. Makes 1 loaf.

GEORGE GOODWIN WALSH (1907-1983) was the husband of MOLLIE WORTHEN OGDEN whom he met and married in 1933. They had two sons (George and Mahlon) and a daughter (Sue Campbell). He was from Alabama, educated at Georgia Tech, and spent over 40 years associated with the Aetna Group Life Insurance Company. After retiring and moving back to Little Rock in 1969 he took up things he had never had time for before, like cooking. This was one of his favorite recipes that has stood the test of time and is just plain good.

Healthy Muffins

1 1/2 cups oat bran

1 cup flaxseed, ground

1 Tbs. baking powder

2 un-peeled oranges,
   quartered and seeded

1/2 cup canola oil

2 eggs

1 1/2 cups golden raisins

1 cup all-purpose flour
   (preferably whole wheat)

1 cup wheat bran

1/2 tsp. salt

1 cup brown sugar

1 cup buttermilk (low fat)

1 tsp. baking soda

Line muffin pans with paper liners or coat with cooking spray. In large bowl combine oat bran, wheat bran, flour, flax seed, baking powder, and salt. Set aside. In blender or food processor combine oranges, brown sugar, canola oil, buttermilk, eggs, and baking soda and blend well. Pour orange mixture into dry ingredients. Mix until well blended. Stir in raisins.

Pre-heat oven to 375 degrees. Bake for 18 to 20 minutes or until toothpick inserted in center comes out clean. Cool in pans 5 minutes before removing to cooling rack. Makes 18 muffins.

MacArthur Park

Originally purchased by the U. S. Government in 1837 for an arsenal, it is now Little Rock's oldest park. In 1890 the government abandoned it and offered it for sale. A group of men purchased the grounds in 1893 for a city park. They removed 28 of the 35 buildings and built a large bandstand and two well houses. In 1933, a fish pond was built by the WPA, and the Fine Arts Building was built in 1936. The Arkansas Arts Center was added in 1963. Today the Arsenal Building is the Arkansas Military Museum, and also home to the Aesthetic Club. In 1942 the park was named MacArthur Park in honor of General Douglas MacArthur, who was born in the Arsenal Building. (Photo below.)

Douglas MacArthur was born in Arkansas because his father, Captain Arthur MacArthur, was stationed in Little Rock and lived with his wife in the Arsenal Building. Mrs. MacArthur became pregnant and selected an army doctor, Dr. Bently, who agreed that it would be safe for her to go back to Virginia to have the baby. However, she had early labor pains, making the trip unadvisable; and Dr. Bently was out of town, so they called in DR. A. L. BREYSACHER. The baby, Douglas, arrived January 26, 1880, without any problems; and Dr. Breysacher signed the necessary papers including the baptismal certificate at Christ Episcopal Church. Although he grew up in Virginia and served, of course, all over the world in his military career, his birthplace was Little Rock, Arkansas.

General and Mrs. MacArthur came to Little Rock on March 23, 1952, for the renaming of the City Park to MacArthur Park. They arrived in time for Sunday service at Christ Church, had lunch with Elsie and Howard Stebbins, and then MacArthur spoke briefly at the bandstand in the park to a large crowd.

Bread Sticks

(Great bread sticks to have on hand for salad, soup or anytime.)

Hamburger buns (or hot dog buns)
(whole wheat may be used)
Caraway seeds

Soft margarine or butter
Parmesan cheese

After slicing buns in strips and buttering, roll in parmesan cheese and caraway seeds and place on cookie sheet. Bake 2 hours at 200 degrees. Store in zip-lock bag or tin.

Another way to make bread sticks:

Hamburger or hot dog buns, sliced

Mix $^1/_2$ butter and $^1/_2$ olive oil and spread on strips. Roll in mixture of garlic salt and Dill weed. Bake in slow oven.

Sweet Potato Biscuits

1 cup all-purpose flour
$^1/_2$ tsp. salt
$^1/_3$ cup shortening (can use butter)
2 Tbs. milk

2 Tbs. baking powder
2 Tbs. sugar
1 cup cooked, mashed sweet potatoes

Combine first 4 ingredients; cut in shortening until mixture resembles coarse meal. Add sweet potatoes and stir until evenly distributed. Sprinkle milk over flour mixture; stir until dry ingredients are moistened.

Turn dough out onto a heavily floured surface; pat to $^1/_2$" thickness. Cut dough with a 2" biscuit cutter. Place biscuits on a lightly greased baking sheet. Bake at 450 degrees for 10 minutes or until lightly browned. Makes 1 dozen.

Artichoke Quiche

1 9" pastry shell

⅓ cup chopped green onion

1 Tbs. flour

⅔ cup milk

1 cup (4 oz.) hot pepper cheese
  cut in small pieces

2 Tbs. butter

2 eggs

1 14 oz. can artichoke hearts,
  well drained & coarsely chopped.

4 oz. grated sharp cheese

Bake pricked pastry shell 12 minutes at 400 degrees.

Remove from oven and reduce temperature to 350 degrees.

In small skillet melt butter and sauté onion. In large bowl beat eggs, flour, and milk together. Stir in artichokes, hot pepper cheese, and all but 3 Tbs. of cheddar cheese and onion-butter mixture. Stir until well blended. Pour in shell and bake for 45 minutes until firm in center. Sprinkle remaining cheese during last 10 minutes of cooking.

Betty Jane Daugherty's Cheese Strata

HAROLD DAUGHERTY was the long time Commodore of the Maumelle Sailing Club. This cheese strata was a good way to start (or end) a day of hard sailing and a nice make-ahead dish for his first mate, B.J.

12 slices white bread	$^3/_4$ lb. sharp cheese
1 (10 oz.) pkg. chopped broccoli, cooked and drained	2 cups diced ham
	6 slightly beaten eggs
2 Tbs. instant dried onion	$^1/_4$ tsp. dry mustard
3 $^1/_2$ cups milk	$^1/_2$ tsp. salt

Cut 12 shapes from bread; fit scraps (crust removed) into greased 13" x 9" x 2" pan. Place cheese in layer over bread; add broccoli, then ham. Sprinkle onion over all. Combine remaining ingredients and pour over all. Arrange shapes on top. Cover and refrigerate overnight or at least 6 hours. Can freeze at this point. Bake uncovered 55 minutes at 325 – 350 degrees. Grate cheese over top and return to oven 5 minutes. Let stand 10 minutes before serving or it will be runny.

Casseroles

MATTHEW CUNNINGHAM, born in Philadelphia in 1784, was a graduate of the Medical School there. He traveled to China and Europe and moved to New Orleans, studying and practicing medicine along the way. He then went back east and married ELIZA WILSON in New York in 1809. They moved to Missouri and finally to Little Rock in 1820.

Eliza, born in Scotland, had married Pierre Bertrand, whose older brother was Count Henri Bertrand, Napoleon's faithful general who followed Napoleon into exile. The Bertrands were a wealthy family, and Pierre traveled to the West Indies to check on his holdings there and was killed in an insurrection in San Domingo. "After a respectable lapse of time" his widow married Cunningham. She was only 20 years old then. She had two children by Bertrand: Arabella Jane and Charles Pierre Bertrand.

There were so few people in Little Rock at first that Matthew couldn't make a living as a doctor, so Eliza took in boarders until the population increased. To fill in the time, Matthew wrote articles for medical journals.

Eliza was the first white woman in Little Rock. MARIA TONCRAY WATKINS came shortly after. There were only two buildings that could be considered houses—both shanties. The children went to Jesse Brown's log house school, called the Little Rock Academy. Charles later read law with Robert Crittenden, and they founded the *Arkansas Advocate* in 1830 in opposition to the *Gazette* and William E. Woodruff.

Matthew was a Mason and the first doctor here, also the first mayor in 1832 when the town council met in his house at Third and Main streets. There is a plaque on the building there for the Cunninghams. He served as Pulaski County coroner and was active in local politics along with being a doctor.

Also buried at Mount Holly are Eliza Cunningham's son, CHESTER ASHLEY CUNNINGHAM, who was born in 1822 and was the first white child born in Little Rock; and Eliza's daughter, ARABELLA JANE BERTRAND, whose tombstone states that she was "successively" married to Lorenzo Clark, JOHN STRONG, and Joseph Newton, although only Strong is buried beside her.

Vegetable Lasagna

10 dried lasagna noodles
  (about 6 ounces – whole wheat)

1 cup grated sweet potato

1 cup fresh okra, caps removed
  and pods thinly sliced

1 can (6 oz.) tomato paste

2 cups small-curd cottage cheese,
  drained

1/4 cup freshly grated Parmesan cheese

Freshly ground black pepper

1 1/2 pounds fresh spinach

2 cups sliced fresh mushrooms

1/2 cup chopped onion

1 Tbs. olive oil

2 cups tomato sauce

1 Tbs. fined chopped fresh oregano

1 lb. mozzarella or Monterey Jack cheese,
  thinly sliced

Coarse salt

Preheat oven to 375 degrees.

In a large saucepan bring 5 quarts of unsalted water to a rapid boil over high heat. Add the lasagna noodles slowly, 2 or 3 at a time. Cook until tender, 8 to 10 minutes, and drain.

In a medium saucepan, heat the olive oil over medium high heat until hot but not smoking. Add the onion and cook, stirring frequently, for 5 minutes or until tender but not browned. Add the mushrooms, okra, sweet potato, and spinach. Add salt and freshly ground pepper to taste. Continue cooking until soft, another 6 to 8 minutes. Add the tomato sauce, tomato paste, and oregano. Stir to combine and heat through. Set aside.

Layer half the lasagna noodles in a well-greased 13"x 9"x2" baking dish. Cover with half the cottage cheese, half the tomato-vegetable mixture, and half the mozzarella or Monterey Jack. Repeat the four layers.

Bake in the preheated oven for 30 to 35 minutes or until the mixture is bubbly and the top is lightly browned. Let stand for 10 to 12 minutes before serving. Sprinkle with freshly grated Parmesan cheese and serve.

Jane Brett's Spaghetti

3 garlic buds, chopped

2 Tbs. bacon drippings

1 can (15 oz.) tomato sauce
   (or chopped tomatoes)

1 Tbs. Beau Monde

2 tsp. bay leaves

2 tsp. oregano

1 Tbs. herb seasoning

1 or 2 cans mushroom pieces

Parmesan cheese

2 large onions, chopped

1 lb. ground beef

3/4 cup water

1 Tbs. chili powder

2 tsp. basil leaves

2 tsp. Rosemary leaves

2 tsp. leaf marjoram

Salt and pepper to taste

Vermicelli

Cook garlic and onion in bacon drippings. Add beef and brown; add tomato sauce or canned tomatoes. Add spices, salt and pepper. Cook slowly in an iron skillet until consistency of mush. Add mushrooms.

Cook vermicelli and drain; add to meat mixture with grated parmesan. Put in baking dish and sprinkle with more grated parmesan. Either heat in 325 degree oven for 1/2 hour or until bubbles; or freeze, defrost, and then heat.

Chicken Tetrazzini

5 lbs. chopped chicken breast (skinless)

1 onion, chopped

2 Tbs. parsley

2 tsp. garlic powder

1 tsp. red pepper

1 cup milk

$1\,^1/_2$ pkgs. (24oz.) spaghetti

$1\,^1/_4$ lb. Velveeta cheese, cut into small pieces

1 red bell pepper, chopped

2 cans cream of mushroom soup

2 tsp. onion powder

1 stick butter

Salt and pepper to taste

Cook chicken until tender. Chop and set aside. (If you use boneless and skinless breasts, add some chicken bouillon cubes to season broth.) Bring broth to boil. Add red bell pepper, onion, parsley, soup, garlic powder, onion powder, red pepper, stick of butter, and spaghetti. Cook until spaghetti is limp. Add cheese and milk. Turn burner down very low. Stir often, but not all the time until cheese is melted. Put chopped chicken into pot and stir. Turn off stove and place in large baking dish. Cover and bake 30 minutes. Serves 10.

This dish is our sexton Steve Adams's favorite that he always brings to the Mount Holly Board's Christmas luncheon. We like it too, and we wanted to share it with you. He asked that it be dedicated to the memory of its originator, Karon Briggs.

Sexton's House

JAMES GASTON WILLIAMSON was born in 1914 in Monticello, Arkansas. He attended Monticello A and M, then graduated from the University of Arkansas at Fayetteville with a BA degree and a Phi Beta Kappa key. He was a Rhodes scholar for three years at Oxford, served in the U.S. army during World War II, then came to Little Rock and joined the Rose Law Firm where he practiced law for 40 years. He was active in the Arkansas Bar Association and served as its president. During the crisis when Governor Faubus closed all public high schools in Little Rock, Williamson was chosen to chair One Hundred Men for Little Rock, a men's auxiliary to the Women's Emergency Committee to Open Our Schools. The groups working together did manage to get the schools open the next year. He was an efficient overachiever, according to one of his friends, and did not condone mediocrity.

WRENETTA WORTHEN WILLIAMSON was born in 1915. After graduation from high school she traveled around the world. She married Gaston Williamson in 1940 and was affiliated with the Colonial Dames of America, Fine Arts Club, Junior League of Little Rock and Mount Holly Cemetery Board.

Wrenetta hated to cook, so she found good recipes for Chicken Spaghetti and Congealed Orange Salad and served them every time she had company. She completed the menu with crackers or bread and ice cream and cookies from the grocery store; and everything was fixed the day before.

Wrenetta's Chicken Spaghetti

2 to 4 lbs. cooked chicken, chopped	1/2 tsp. garlic, chopped
1 can (14 oz.) cut tomatoes	4 oz. can (or fresh) mushrooms
1 tsp. Worcestershire	1/2 green pepper, chopped
3 Tbs. flour dissolved in water	1 cup chopped black olives with juice
2 cups chicken broth	16 oz. cheddar cheese, grated
1 onion	12 oz. cooked spaghetti

In a large Dutch oven brown chopped onion and garlic in 2 Tbs. butter. Add can of tomatoes, mushrooms, green pepper, chicken broth and 1 Tbs. Worcestershire sauce.

Thicken with the flour/water mixture. Cook for 30 minutes in a slow simmer. Season to taste. Add chicken and chopped black olives to the sauce. In a 3 qt. casserole alternate layers of chicken sauce, spaghetti, and cheese. Top last layer with cheese. Heat in 350 degree oven for 30 minutes.

Meat

THE GEORGE BROTHERS–ALEXANDER, HENRY, WILLIAM, AND LOUIE–came to Little Rock in 1833 from Germany. They were energetic entrepreneurs who successfully mastered the frontier town environment. Among many diverse enterprises and civic activities, they operated a beer garden for decades in downtown Little Rock. An advertisement in the *Arkansas Gazette* announced the opening of the Little Rock City Garden "for the reception of visitors, both during the day and evening." They also opened a brewery that likely made some of the refreshments served at the City Garden. Other enterprises included a banking operation, general merchandise store, and a trading operation with a barge that traveled the Arkansas River many miles above and below Little Rock–supplying farmers, planters, and merchants with everything they needed.

George Brother's Biergarten Franks

2 lbs. pre-cooked German-style frankfurters

1 12 oz. bottle of pilsner beer

1 large can or medium bag of sauerkraut

1 tart apple, diced

Place sauerkraut and diced apple in bottom of Crockpot or Dutch oven. Cover with frankfurters and add beer. Simmer for 4-6 hours. Drain. Serve with pickled beets, and garnish franks with German mustard. If uncooked sausages such as bratwurst are substituted, boil on high heat for 45 minutes, and then reduce to low.

After the Civil War, Louie moved to Reid's Landing, seven miles below what is now Scott, with his son William. Their plan was to found a town to be called Georgetown, but after the death of both Louie and William, the town never became a reality, but the lake was named Georgetown Lake.

ALEXANDER GEORGE accumulated enough wealth during the 1850's to allow him to live sumptuously for the rest of his life. In 1837 he invested in undeveloped land. When he was only 29 years old in 1841, he was elected alderman. He served again as alderman in 1849 and was swept from office in 1855 by the Know Nothing Party. Ironically, one of Alexander's fellow aldermen during his first term in 1841 had been Albert Pike, leader of the Know Nothing Party in Arkansas.

Little Rock was occupied by the Union Army in 1863 and for two and a half years was without an elected municipal government. When a Common Council was finally elected in 1866, Alexander was on the panel. This group had the task of reconstructing local government in Little Rock. During its first few months it passed a series of ordinances which re-established basic fire and police services, regulated health and safety of the city and re-imposed municipal taxes.

In 1858-59 Alexander constructed a two-story Georgian style home on East 2nd Street between Byrd and McLean Streets. The George House, one of a half dozen antebellum homes was built out of hand-made brick with walls 15" to 24" thick. There were sculptured gardens stretching from the veranda of his house to the Arkansas River with a boardwalk from the house to the river. Boats would tie up to the bank to allow passengers to go ashore and stroll through the gardens. (The Clinton Presidential Library is at this site today.)

Alexander helped found the German Lutheran Church and school, which is still standing on the corner of 8th and Rock Streets. His funeral was held at the church and was said to have been one of the largest ever witnessed in the city.

WILLIAM (BILL) GEORGE and his father Louie moved to Scott after Bill won land on the Arkansas River, near Scott, in a poker game. When Bill came back from the Civil War he married Ellen Dailey, built a house at Georgetown and soon after was killed by either a carpetbagger or a disgruntled poker player—maybe both. Bill, a descendent of one of the earliest fathers of Little Rock, was described as a tall, handsome, red-headed, riverboat gambler. His descendents still own property on Georgetown Lake at Scott.

One of the most interesting people buried at Mount Holly is WILLIAM S. FULTON. He was appointed Governor of the Arkansas Territory by President Andrew Jackson and presided over the territory until Arkansas was admitted into the Union in 1836. The first legislature that met under the new state's government named Fulton as one of Arkansas's first U. S. Senators. He was re-elected in 1840 and served until his death.

He died at his home, Rosewood, on August 15, 1844, after a ten-day illness attributed to sleeping in a freshly painted room. Rosewood later became an industrial school, and today is the site of the Governor's Mansion. Fulton County is named for him.

Arkansas Governor's Mansion

Meat Loaf

1 lb. ground beef

½ cup milk

¼ cup finely chopped parsley

½ tsp. freshly ground pepper

½ cup chopped onion

    (sauté onion and garlic in 3 Tbs. butter)

½ tsp. oregano

¼ tsp. fennel seeds (or marjoram)

½ cup fresh bread crumbs

1 lightly beaten egg

1 tsp. salt

½ tsp. paprika

1 minced garlic clove

½ tsp. basil

Top with Tomato-Basil Sauce

Preheat oven to 425 degrees. Bake ½ hour, then pour ½ cup beef broth over and bake another ½ hour at 350 degrees.

Tomato—Basil Sauce

6 large fresh tomatoes

3 Tbs. extra-virgin olive oil

¼ tsp. kosher salt

2 garlic cloves, chopped

⅓ cup chopped fresh basil

Coarsely ground black pepper

Chop tomatoes and place in a bowl. Add garlic, olive oil, basil, salt and pepper. Toss gently. Cover with plastic wrap and let stand at room temperature 2 to 4 hours.

Brunswick Stew

A 25 cent shank of beef*

1 qt. potatoes, cooked and mashed

1 qt. raw corn scraped
with its milk from cob

A 5 cent loaf of bread

1 qt. cooked butter beans

1 $^1/_2$ qts. raw tomatoes, peeled and chopped

If served for dinner (noon time) put on the shank as for soup in $^1/_2$ gallon of water at the earliest possible hour; then simmer lightly. About 4 hours later take the shank out of the soup, shred and cut all of the meat as fine as possible, carefully taking out bone and gristle, then return meat to the soup pot and add all the vegetables and two slices of middling (salt pork or smoked side meat). Season with salt and pepper to taste. When ready to serve drop in 2 or 3 Tbs. of butter.

*(The shank of beef and loaf of bread may cost more now.)

(Squirrel and chicken also make a good stew.)

By October 1835 there was a lot of discussion about becoming a state, and there were strong feelings about it. Ambrose Sevier and several of his like-minded pro-statehood friends met at the Grog Shop in Hinderliter Tavern to discuss the matter over Brunswick Stew.

AMBROSE SEVIER settled in Little Rock in 1821 and became one of the founders of a political dynasty that ruled antebellum Arkansas politics from the 1820's until the Civil War. When Sevier's cousin, territorial delegate Henry W. Conway, was killed in a duel in 1827, Sevier assumed leadership of the family. He was elected territorial delegate in a special election and took his seat in Congress in February, 1828. His political faction evolved into Arkansas's Democratic Party.

Sevier secured Arkansas's bid for statehood, with President Andrew Jackson signing the bill—making it the 25th state on June 15, 1836. Arkansas's first legislature rewarded Sevier by electing him as one of the state's first two U. S. Senators. During his twelve-year tenure he chaired two major committees: Indian Affairs and Foreign Relations.

Beef Stew

2 lbs. of beef	2 onions, chopped
4 potatoes, roughly chopped	2 carrots, chopped
2 stalks celery, chopped	Salt and pepper

Cut beef into cubes. Lay half in bottom of saucepan. Work half carrots through the beef, then a layer of onions and potatoes over the beef and season. Mix the remaining carrots, celery, and beef and place as the next layer. Top with a layer of onions and potatoes and season. Just cover with water, sprinkle with herbs and simmer for an hour and a half.

Serves 4.

Three brothers—D. F., D. G., AND JAMES FONES—organized the Fones Brothers Hardware Company. The brothers had faith in the future of Little Rock as an industrial center and built one of the most complete and best arranged buildings of its kind in the state. It covered four lots and was five stories with a basement and total floor space of over 160,000 square feet. Built of reinforced concrete, it was fireproof and further protected by a Globe automatic sprinkler system. Today that building has been restored as the Main Library at Second and Rock Streets. (Photo below.)

Fire Alarm Chili

3 Tbs. bacon grease

2 cloves garlic

2 Tbs. chili powder

1 cup tomato sauce

$1/2$ tsp. celery seed

1 small bay leaf

$1 1/2$ tsp. salt

1 large onion

1 lb. ground beef

1 can (6 oz.) tomato paste

1 bell pepper, minced

$1/4$ tsp. ground cumin

Pinch basil

1 cup cooked beans

In a large skillet, cook meat, onion, and garlic until meat has lost red color. Add remaining ingredients, mixing well. Cover and simmer for one hour. Yield: 2 $1/2$ qts.

Purists Chili

2 Tbs. bacon grease

2 lbs. cubed beef

$1/4$ tsp. garlic

1 cup water

Salt to taste

1 - 4 Tbs. flour

2 Tbs. minced onion

2 - 3 Tbs. chili powder

$1/2$ tsp. ground cumin

Dredge the meat cubes in flour. Heat bacon grease and brown meat. Stir in onion and garlic. Add chili powder, then water and cumin. Bring to boil and salt to taste. Simmer covered two or three hours, until meat is tender.

Firemen who died in the line of duty are commemorated on several tombstones including those of ROBERT YEAKLE, who died in 1892 when he tried to jump aboard a moving fire wagon and was crushed as he fell beneath the rear wheel; and JAMES ROBINS, who died in 1895 fighting a fire that destroyed the town's Methodist Church. Robins "was borne to the cemetery on a hearse improvised with pride from one of the hose reels belonging to the fire company of which he was captain." The most imposing fireman's monument, and a favorite of school children, is the statue of HENRY BROOKIN. He has a fire helmet on his head and a hose in his hands as he stands, obviously ready for action, on a granite column that tells how he died in 1891, age 35, "answering an alarm of fire."

Brisket

1 (5 lb.) beef brisket

1 Tbs. olive oil

1 lb. coarsely chopped onion
(about 4 medium)

1 bay leaf

$^{1}/_{2}$ cup low-sodium soy sauce

4 slices crustless rye bread cubed (optional)

12 oz. tomato paste

Coarsely ground black pepper and salt

$^{1}/_{4}$ cup diced garlic (about 12 cloves)

1 bottle burgundy wine

1 tsp. fresh rosemary

$^{2}/_{3}$ cup water

Preheat oven to 350 degrees.

Heat oil in a large skillet until hot. Add meat and sear over high heat until lightly browned. Then rub brisket with tomato paste, salt, and pepper.

Place onions in a large roasting pan. Place meat, fat side up, on top of onions. Combine garlic, wine, bay leaf, thyme, rosemary, soy sauce, and water. Whisk and pour over brisket. Cover and bake 2 $^{1}/_{2}$ to 3 hours, basting often with pan juices. Uncover, add rye bread (if desired) and bake 30 minutes, until brisket is fork tender. Serves 12.

WILLIAM READ MILLER, the first native-born governor of Arkansas, was born November 23, 1823, on a farm near Batesville, Arkansas Territory. Described by a friend as "a charitable, public-spirited, plain, unassuming gentleman," he served several years as State Auditor but was removed by Reconstruction. He was admitted to the bar in 1868. In 1876 he was nominated by the Democrats to succeed Governor Garland as governor when he advanced to the senate and won. He encouraged black voters and worked to improve Arkansas's poor financial standing. He was committed to public education and the establishment of the University of Arkansas, which gave him an honorary doctorate degree. He died in Little Rock in 1887.

JAMES MITCHELL was born in 1832 at Cane Hill (Washington County). He was educated at Cane Hill College, the oldest chartered institution of learning in the state. Mitchell dropped out of college at the age of 15, and for the next ten years he alternated farming (to make money) with teaching and studying, his true love. From 1855 to 1859 he was United States Deputy Surveyor to survey Kansas and Nebraska. He married Sarah Elizabeth Latta, returned to teaching, then served in the state legislature before volunteering as private in the Confederate army in 1861. When he left the army in 1865 as Captain, he resumed farming and teaching until he became chairman of the English Literature Department of the Arkansas Industrial University at Fayetteville, now the University of Arkansas.

Mitchell left teaching in 1876 to become editor-in-chief of the *Arkansas Gazette*, surprising some of his friends; but he said: "The newspaper is continuing education." In 1878 he bought the evening newspaper, the *Arkansas Democrat*, and continued his interest in education. He said: "Educate the people, elevate the image of the state."

SARAH ELIZABETH LATTA MITCHELL (Mrs. James Mitchell) was born in 1839 at Evansville, Arkansas. Concerned about children whose parents died during the war, she started the Orphans Home in Little Rock soon after the war. The name was later changed to the Elizabeth Mitchell Home and was later merged with other agencies to form The Centers for Youth and Families. The need has shifted from orphans to troubled children, and the Mitchell family has continued its interest in the organization through the years.

Lemon—Herb Pot Roast

3 to 3 ½ pound boneless beef chuck pot roast

2 cloves garlic, crushed

1 tsp. dried basil

2 Tbs. cornstarch,
    dissolved in 2 Tbs. water

2 tsp. lemon pepper

1 Tbs. olive oil

½ tsp. dried basil

VEGETABLES:

2 cups peeled baby carrots

1 medium onion, cut into wedges

1 lb. small red potatoes, cut in half

Combine garlic, lemon pepper, and 1 tsp. basil; press evenly into surface of beef. In Dutch oven, heat oil over medium-high heat until hot. Brown beef evenly. Pour off drippings. Add 1 cup water. Bring to a boil; reduce heat to low. Cover tightly; simmer 2 hours.

Add vegetables; cover and continue cooking 40 to 45 minutes or until beef and vegetables are tender. Remove beef and vegetables.

Skim fat from cooking liquid. Stir in cornstarch mixture and ½ tsp. basil. Bring to a boil; cook and stir until thickened. Serve sauce with pot roast and vegetables. Makes 6 servings.

ERNEST FENNELL, born in 1919, was the Insurance Commissioner for Arkansas and also an ordained Episcopal priest. He and his wife, BEVERLY, started St. Francis House in Little Rock, then
moved to Chicago and retired in Franklin, Tennessee in 1972. There they ran a cooking school and
herb farm called Hyssop Hill until his death in 1992. This Pepper Steak recipe was one of Ernie's
favorites.

Pepper Steak

1 chuck roast – 2 inches thick

2 tsp. meat tenderizer – sprinkle on sides of meat and pierce with fork.

Marinade: 2 Tbs. instant minced onion, 2 tsp. thyme, 1 tsp. marjoram, 1 bay leaf crushed, 1 cup red wine
vinegar, $^1/_2$ cup olive oil, 3 Tbs. lemon juice. Pour over steak and marinate 1 hour or more. Drain.

Pound $^1/_4$ cup cracked pepper into steak with mallet. Cook 15 minutes (for rare in the middle) on each
side, over medium heat on grill. Cut thin slices against grain.

Serves 16.

Spiced Apple Butter Pork Roast

3 1/2 lb. boneless, center-cut lean pork loin roast or boneless lean pork sirloin roast

1 (1 lb., 13 oz.) jar apple butter (about 2 1/3 cups)

1/4 cup apple brandy or apple juice	2 Tbs. apple juice
2 Tbs. cider vinegar	2 Tbs. lemon juice
2 Tbs. prepared horseradish	1 tsp. Dijon mustard
1/4 tsp. salt	1/4 tsp. coarsely ground pepper

Place roast in a sealable plastic bag. In a bowl, combine apple butter with brandy (if used), apple juice, vinegar, lemon juice, horseradish, mustard, salt and pepper; stir well. Reserve 2 cups apple-butter mixture, cover and chill. Pour remaining apple-butter mixture over roast; seal bag and marinate in refrigerator 8 hours.

Heat oven to 350 degrees. Line a shallow roasting pan with heavy-duty foil. Remove roast from bag; place roast in prepared pan and drizzle with marinade. Insert meat thermometer into thickest portion of roast. Bake until meat thermometer registers pork setting (pork will be slightly pink). Place reserved 2 cups apple-butter mixture in a small saucepan. Place over low heat and heat thoroughly. Serve with roast.

Makes 12 ample servings.

GILBERT KNAPP was born in 1827 in Erie, Pennsylvania; and MARY ELIZA FIELD KNAPP was born in 1825 in Tennessee. Mrs. Knapp's first husband, William P. Officer, owned the land with the Toltec Mounds south of Little Rock. Later she married Gilbert Knapp, who also had extensive holdings in Pulaski and Lonoke counties and who managed the Mounds. Mr. Knapp determined that the mounds had been built by the Toltecs; but when the Smithsonian Institution inspected them, they said the Toltecs never did come this far north. The wrong name stuck, and the builders have not been definitely identified.

Mrs. Knapp was a charter member of the Aesthetic Club in 1883 and was also their mentor since she was in her fifties and the others were in their twenties and thirties. She belonged to Christ Church, the only Episcopal Church in town. However, she supported Bishop Pierce, who had stayed with the Knapps when his family first came to Little Rock, in founding Trinity Cathedral. He had offered the title of cathedral to Christ Church, but they declined.

When she died she left $1,000 to Christ Church and $1,000 to Trinity Cathedral for each to have a marble alter. However, Christ Church used its gift for a large transept window (the church burned in 1938); and Trinity used its windfall for carved pews, which are still in use. She also left some money to the city to build a drinking fountain in what is now MacArthur Park because that was approximately half way between downtown and where many residents lived on the east side, and they usually got thirsty walking that distance. The fountain is still there, but it was moved to a spot behind the Arsenal building.

Leg of Lamb

Pierce lamb several times and fill with slivers of garlic (if you are in a hurry, rub all over with garlic powder) and dried rosemary. Sprinkle with a teaspoon of sugar, salt and pepper to taste. Roast uncovered in 325 – 350 degree oven for 2 or 3 hours. If it gets dry, add a little water or broth to make au jus.

Mary Worthen says this is how her mother, Mamie Fletcher, cooked lamb.

WILLIAM E. WOODRUFF, SR. was a loyal apprentice for a printer in Brooklyn after the death of his father. The original contract of indenture bears the date October 18, 1810, and is on exhibit in the Historic Arkansas Museum. At age 14 he bound himself for six years to his master to faithfully serve; his secrets keep; and "at cards, dice, or any other unlawful games, he shall not play; taverns or ale-houses he shall not frequent ..."

In 1817 he set out for the west to seek his fortune. It was then a rugged trip to go to Wheeling, Virginia; but he made it successfully, and he and a companion apprentice purchased a skiff and descended the Ohio to the falls, now Louisville, Kentucky. Here he remained some months, then walked to Russellville, Kentucky, and to Nashville and Franklin, Tennessee. In Tennessee he worked in companionship with Henry Van Pelt, who later founded the *Memphis Appeal.* When he heard of the creation of the Arkansas Territory in 1819, with Arkansas Post as the capital, he decided to start a newspaper there.

He arrived in the new territory on October 30, 1819 with a printing outfit, and on November 20, 1819 founded the *Arkansas Gazette* by bringing out the first issue of a newspaper printed west of the Mississippi. He continued to edit the newspaper until 1838 when he sold it. In 1841 the paper reverted back to him and he sold it again in 1843. In 1846, finding it impossible to remain out of the newspaper business, he established the *Arkansas Democrat* and in 1850 again bought the *Gazette* and consolidated the *Democrat* with it. In March 1853 he sold the newspaper to C. C. Danley and retired permanently.

In 1836 Mr. Woodruff was elected by the first State Legislature to the office of State Treasurer. He also wrote Arkansas's first book entitled Laws of the Territory of Arkansas. He was married to JANE ELIZA MILLS and was the father of 11 children.

Upon his death in 1885, the paper wrote: "The influence exerted by Mr. Woodruff during a third of a century, through the *Gazette,* and by virtue of his strong personal force, far exceeded that of any other influence in the state. Always at the front, battling for democracy; always ready to espouse the cause of a valued friend; a hard hitter who could give and sustain heavy blows; always laboring in behalf of every measure calculated to advance the state of his adoption, he wielded a power that could hardly be over-estimated. His history is a part of the history of Arkansas, and his name will live as long as her history shall be written and read and remembered."

Baked Liver with Bacon

Cut fresh beef liver into thick slices and lay in a baking pan. Upon each slice of liver place strips of bacon, a liberal amount of chopped onion, and a few strips of green pepper. Sprinkle with salt, pepper, and paprika. Add 1 cup water and bake slowly for 1 hour.

Woodruff family recipe.

Woodruff's printing press at
Historic Arkansas Museum

JOSEF ROSENBERG made his piano debut at the age of nine in a Budapest concert hall. His music career brought him from his Hungarian homeland to Little Rock where he came to fill a post in musical instruction offered at the "Institute of Art and Expression." Although the Institute did not last, Rosenberg stayed and for almost 60 years taught piano and voice to hundreds of Arkansans.

Hungarian Goulash

3 Tbs. oil

1 medium size onion, finely chopped

1 Tbs. sweet or hot paprika

1 green pepper, cored, seeded
   and cut in 4 pieces

1/4 tsp. caraway seeds

Salt and pepper

1 1/2 lbs. boneless chuck steak, cut in 1" cubes

1 clove garlic, finely chopped

1 cup water or enough to cover ingredients

1 medium tomato, seeded
   and cut in 4 pieces

5 medium size potatoes, peeled and diced

Heat oil and brown the beef, a few pieces at a time, until browned on all sides. Remove beef and add the onion and garlic. Cook for 3 minutes and return the beef to the pan. Add the paprika, water, green pepper, tomato, caraway seeds, salt and pepper. Cover and cook over very low heat for 1 1/2 to 2 hours. Add the potatoes and cook 30 minutes more. Serve with Csipetke. Recipe follows.

Csipetke

6 Tbs. flour

2 Tbs. water

1 whole egg

1/4 tsp. salt

Measure flour onto the counter. Make a well in the center and add the egg, water and salt. Knead with your fingertips until a firm dough is formed. Roll the dough into a rectangle 1/2" thick. Cut into strips 1" x 1 1/2" and roll into cylinders in the palm of your hand. Simmer the dough cylinders in hot soup for 30 minutes and serve in soup as a garnish.

Poultry & Game

Parmesan Chicken

Mix in blender:

1 cup corn flakes	$^1/_2$ cup parmesan cheese	$^3/_4$ tsp. garlic salt
2 or 3 tsp. parsley	1 tsp. salt	

Melt stick of butter and add 1 or 2 drops of sesame oil. Dip chicken pieces in butter and roll in mixture. Place on baking sheet and bake at 350 degrees for 1 hour and 15 minutes.

Baked Chicken Breasts

Wash and dry chicken breasts. Salt a little and then sprinkle both sides with garlic salt and paprika. Mix 1 cup of heavy cream and 1 can mushroom soup and pour over chicken. Sprinkle parsley on top. Bake uncovered at 350 degrees for 1 $^1/_2$ hours.

COL. SANDY FAULKNER came to Arkansas in 1829 and settled in Chicot County, on the Mississippi River, as a cotton planter. In 1839 he took up residence in Little Rock on the Arkansas River. He was proud to be the original personator of the "Arkansas Traveler." A grand banquet was given in the famous "Barroom" which used to stand near the Anthony House. Col. Sandy was called on to play the tune and tell the story. Afterward it grew in popularity. When he subsequently went to New Orleans, the fame of "Arkansas Traveler" had gone before him; and at a banquet amid clinking glasses and brilliant toasts, he was handed a violin by the (then) governor of Louisiana and requested to favor them with the favorite Arkansas tune. At the old St. Charles hotel a special room was devoted to his use, bearing in gilt letters over the door, "Arkansas Traveler." His tombstone includes a few bars from "The Arkansas Traveler."

Basil & Lemon Chicken

In large bowl, mix $1/2$ cup each of chopped spring onions and basil leaves. Add juice of 1 lemon, salt and pepper. Mix and rub into chicken breasts and place in well-oiled baking pan. Dribble with a little olive oil. Roast uncovered at 350 degrees for 30 minutes or until done. Garnish with more basil leaves and lemon slices. Serves 6.

Chicken Breasts with Mushroom Sauce

Flour, salt and pepper 8 chicken breasts and brown them in butter. Sauté 1 lb. fresh mushrooms. Place mushrooms over chicken breasts in a casserole dish. Mix together: 1 carton sour cream, $1/2$ cup dry white wine, and a pinch of rosemary. Pour mixture over chicken and bake for $1 1/4$ hours or until done.

ANNE HUNT BOND (Mrs. Will Bond) was a delightful person, a loyal friend, and a good cook who loved to entertain. She was also good company and always "pepped up" any gathering. Her daughters shared this recipe with us.

Anne Bond's Chicken Spectacular

3 whole cooked chicken breasts

1 medium onion, chopped

Small jar of pimentos

1 cup Hellman's mayonnaise

1 box Uncle Ben's $\frac{1}{2}$ white and $\frac{1}{2}$ wild rice, prepare as directed

1 can water chestnuts, chopped

1 can cream of celery soup

Cube chicken and combine with rice and the rest of ingredients. Bake 30 minutes at 350 degrees, until bubbly.

JOHN GOULD FLETCHER was an art authority, lecturer, author, and poet. A founder of the Arkansas Folklore Society and Arkansas Historical Society, he was the author of a major state history published in 1947, and a Pulitzer Prize winner (1939) for Selected Poems—the first poet south of the Mason-Dixon line to be so honored. In 1939, John Gould and Charlie May were living at Remembrance Farm House (known now as Butterfield House) by Pinnacle Mountain without a phone because he didn't want to be disturbed while writing. When he won the Pulitzer, the press couldn't reach him and asked "Uncle" Bob Butterfield, who owned the place, to go with them to help them find it so they could notify him. When they got there and John Gould opened the door, he said, "Bob, I told you I didn't want any company."

CHARLIE MAY HOGUE FLETCHER was most famous for her children's books written under the nom de plume of Charlie May Simon. She was probably the state's most prolific major author, writing 17 books in a career that began in 1934 with the publication of Robin on the Mountain, still considered a classic in children's literature. She was a prize-winning biographer, and her subjects ranged from philosopher-musician- physician Albert Schweitzer to the crown prince and princess of Japan. Her last book, published in 1974, was Faith Has Need of All the Truth, a biography of French priest Telhand de Chardin. For her children's books—and for some of her more "adult" work as well—Mrs. Fletcher drew heavily on her knowledge and love of Arkansas.

Chicken Pie

4 to 5 lb. chicken or chicken breasts

1 onion, diced

1 sprig parsley, chopped

$1\,^{1}/_{2}$ tsp. salt

5 Tbs. flour

$^{1}/_{2}$ cup tiny peas

$^{1}/_{4}$ lb. butter

1 carrot, diced

1 stalk celery, chopped

1 tsp. rosemary

$^{3}/_{8}$ tsp. pepper

1 cup cream

4 oz. can sliced mushrooms

Pie crust, unbaked

Clean and disjoint chicken. Place on a rack in pan half-filled with hot water. Add the carrot, onion, celery, parsley, rosemary, $^{1}/_{2}$ tsp. of the salt, and $^{1}/_{8}$ tsp. of the pepper. Partly cover the pan with a lid. Simmer the chicken for 3 to 4 hours, until it is tender. Turn it occasionally. Cool chicken, breast side down in broth in pan. When cool, skim off fat and strain broth. In saucepan blend flour with $^{1}/_{4}$ cup broth from chicken. Slowly stir in another $1\,^{1}/_{4}$ cups broth. Add cream. Cook until sauce thickens. Stir constantly to avoid lumps. Season with remaining 1 tsp. salt and $^{1}/_{4}$ tsp. pepper. Bone and cut meat into pieces and add to sauce. Add peas, carrots, mushrooms and butter. Put into a baking dish. Cover with pie dough. Press pastry against side of dish. Cut gashes across top of the pastry. Bake 425 degrees for 12 to 15 minutes.

Serves 6.

A native of Austria, PETER HOTZE is buried beneath an ornate cross with the anthemion design (floral cluster) on top—a popular Victorian tombstone style found in cemeteries from New Orleans to New England. Peter came to Little Rock in the 1850s and became the ultimate Southerner—serving in the Confederate Army and going into business with John Gould Fletcher, Sr. as a cotton broker. As their business expanded, Hotze was required to live in New York City for several years but returned to Little Rock where he built an Italianate home that was his show place for his latter years. Like true Southern gentlemen, Hotze and Fletcher met at the beginning of each year, divided the previous year's profits evenly, and shook hands on the partnership. Nothing was ever written—just a hand-shake.

LAURA WOOLDRIDGE HOPSON, a descendant of the Hotze family, was married to WILLIAM D. HOPSON, a World War II aviator with the Flying Tigers, who had a distinguished career in the Air Force. They had no children, so she went with him everywhere she could; and wherever it was offered, she took a Cardon Bleu cooking course.

Hot Chicken Salad

2 cups diced cooked chicken breasts	1 can mushroom soup
3/4 cup mayonnaise	1/2 cup diced celery
1/2 cup diced green pepper	1 cup rice, cooked in chicken broth
1 Tbs. lemon juice	1 Tbs. grated onion
3 1/2 oz. can sliced mushrooms, drained	1/2 cup sliced almonds
2 Tbs. butter	

Mix chicken, soup, mayonnaise, celery, bell pepper, rice, lemon, and all other ingredients in greased casserole. Sprinkle with almonds and bake at 350 degrees until thoroughly hot.

Quail

1 $^1/_2$ quarts water, seasoned with 1 tsp. each garlic powder, onion powder, salt, and pepper

2 quail per person

Drop frozen quail into boiling seasoned water. Return to boil, reduce to simmer, cover and cook for 5 minutes. Let sit until ready to serve (do this several hours ahead). At serving time, make sauce of 8 oz. melted butter, 6 oz. teriyaki sauce, salt, pepper, garlic powder, and onion powder. Remove birds from water and let rest in sauce 10-20 minutes. Then grill for 45 seconds to 1 minute. Serve them on thin-sliced country ham and a slice of toast.

This quail recipe of LAURA CAMPBELL NICHOLS is an elegant presentation, as well as delicious.

MARIA KEATTS THIBAULT journeyed from Virginia to Arkansas with her family around 1831. The journey from Memphis to Little Rock was especially arduous, as just a primitive road (called the Old Military Road) existed through the wilderness. Even in good conditions, the trip required as much as 20 days by wagon. They fell in about a day's journey behind a group of Cherokee and Choctaw Indians in order to use the Indians' deserted campsites the following night.

They settled on Fourche Island, east of Little Rock, where Maria's father took up three land grants of 1,000 acres each and built a home for his family. In 1839 Maria married Felix Thibault, a young man who had also arrived in Arkansas around 1831. Wild game was plentiful and was a main source of food for the Thibault family. Once in a day's hunt two bears, a wolf, four wild cats, and some deer were brought home as bounty. The men rose at daybreak, breakfasted at sunrise on fried venison and pork, corn dodgers, and coffee, and then sallied forth to hunt—returning usually at supper-time.

Felix was an adventurer with a touch of the wanderlust. He left his wife and children for two years in search of gold and wealth in California. He returned home and fathered two more children. However, soon after the youngest was born, he had Albert Pike arrange for a divorce—a very unusual occurrence in those days. Felix left Arkansas and started a new family in New Orleans.

Maria, with the help of her family—especially her brother, JAMES BUFORD KEATTS—raised her children and managed her own land located near the Keatts plantation on Fourche Island. She died in 1864, five weeks after her oldest son was killed in a Civil War battle. A tombstone in memory of both Maria and her son, HENRY KEATTS, was erected by James Buford Keatts and placed in the Keatts lot.

Wild Duck and Dressing

Stuff wild duck with following:

Cut-up apple, potato, onion, and celery. Salt and pepper well.

Place in roasting pan with 1 pint water and 3-4 bay leaves. Bake in moderate oven for 3 hours or until tender. Remove duck and set aside. Save remaining broth & discard rest of contents.

DRESSING:

Equal parts baked cornbread and toasted breads crumbled together. Add chopped nuts, onion, and celery to proportion. Stir in broth until mixture is soupy. Whip in 6-8 eggs, 2 Tbs. sage, salt and pepper to taste. Pour into greased container. Bake covered for one hour in moderate oven. Uncover to brown.

JAMES TAPPAN HORNOR from Helena, Arkansas, was an insurance executive, active in the business world and an avid hunter and fisherman. He not only shot and caught his wild game; he also cooked it. Here is his Wild Duckling recipe:

Wild Duckling

2 ducks

1/2 cup butter

4-oz can mushroom and liquid

1 pod garlic

1 onion, chopped

1 bell pepper, chopped

1 pkg. Pepperidge Farm dressing

Salt and pepper

Place ducks in Dutch oven with butter, garlic, mushrooms, onion, and bell pepper. Salt and pepper generously. Cover and cook on low heat for 2 1/2 to 3 1/2 hours. Remove ducks and carve. Add dressing to juices and mix well. Serve together. Serves 4 - 6

The Folsom Mausoleum was restored in 1978 with a $3,000 grant from the Caduceus Club as a commemorative project for the Medical School's centennial.

Seafood

Tap Hornor's Rainbow Trout

Split cleaned trout and lay open on aluminum foil. Dot with butter. Add salt, pepper, and slices of lemon. Add lots of paprika sprinkled on top. Broil 12 minutes four inches below flame.

Baked Catfish

4 large catfish filets

Season well with salt and pepper. Put on top of each other to make a loaf and bake 20 minutes in 350 degree oven. Remove. Coat with Hellmann's mayo and pat crushed Ritz crackers all over top and sides. Bake 30 minutes in 350 degree oven. Top with slices of lemon. D. Campbell

(Suggestion: You can use Club crackers or panka and add herbs such as parsley, chives, or fennel.)

Oysters Delmonico

4 slices bacon, diced

2 shallots, minced

1/4 cup minced green pepper

Dash cayenne pepper

2 lbs. rock salt

1 1/2 Tbs. lemon juice

2 Tbs. butter plus 1 tsp. butter, divided

1/4 cup minced red bell pepper

Dash salt

1/4 cup bread crumbs

12 oysters on the half shell

Fry bacon in a small skillet over medium heat until crisp, 3 to 4 minutes. Drain and crumble. Melt 2 Tbs. butter in saucepan, add shallots and bell peppers and cook until softened. Season with salt and cayenne to taste. In separate skillet, melt remaining tsp. butter over low heat. Add bread crumbs, stir to combine, and remove from heat.

Heat oven to 375 degrees. Fill jelly roll pan with rock salt to about 1/2 inch deep. Arrange oysters on pan. Cover them with bacon and vegetable mixture, sprinkle with lemon juice, and top with the bread crumbs. Bake oysters until heated through, 8 minutes. Then place under broiler to lightly brown the bread crumbs, about 1 minute.

JAMES FLEMING FAGAN, whose father was a contractor for the Old State House, was born in Winchester, Kentucky, in 1828, served in the Mexican War, and was promoted to Major General in the Civil War. A family anecdote tells of General Fagan, his wife and children having dinner at Delmonico's restaurant; and very hot oysters were served as the first course. When Mrs. Fagan put the first oyster in her mouth, it was so hot that it made her tear up; but she was afraid to spit it out for fear of committing a faux pas. After a minute or two of this agony, General Fagan, who had noticed her red face and streaming eyes, commanded her to "Spit the damn thing out!"

The oldest monument at Mount Holly, a headless bust dated Roman before 79 AD, is that of MOISE B. SELIGMAN III. He was a graduate of the New York School of Interior Design with his own interior design business in Little Rock. He had bought the bust on a summer trip to Italy. His grandmother's Salmon Loaf was his favorite "comfort food."

Lucille Seligman's Salmon Loaf

1 14 oz. can pink salmon	1 stick butter
3 eggs	Saltine crackers, lots of these crumbled
Salt and pepper to taste	Dash cayenne pepper

Drain salmon, saving the juice, into bowl. Flake with fork. In separate bowl, use saved juice and add beaten eggs, melted butter, salt, pepper, and cayenne. Mix with flaked salmon and add saltine "crumbs" to thicken. Mold into shape. Place in double boiler and boil until firm.

TOP WITH WHITE CREAM SAUCE:

3 Tbs. butter	2 Tbs. minced onion
3 Tbs. flour	1 1/2 cups scalded milk
Salt and white pepper to taste	(heat just until bubbles form around edge of pan)
Pinch of parsley (optional)	

Melt butter over medium heat, add onion and sauté until transparent, about 4–5 minutes. Stir in flour and stir occasionally, cook until bubbly but not browned, about 3 minutes. Whisk in the milk all at once. Season with salt and pepper. Reduce the heat to low and simmer until thick, about 10 minutes. Strain through a sieve, then stir in parsley. Pour over salmon loaf.

ANNE WATKINS WALKER, the daughter of DR. CLAIBOURNE WATKINS, was an early officer of the Mount Holly Board and one of a family of True Grits. Her husband, ROBERT WOODS WALKER, was born at Elmwood Plantation in 1860 and died in 1920 around the end of the Spanish Flu Pandemic. Annie then supplemented the family income with a variety of ventures that included taking in maiden lady boarders, making beautiful birthday and wedding cakes, and one year baking 1,000 pounds of fruitcake from October to December, which she sold for $1.00 a pound—a significant amount at the time.

Annie's daughter Mildred taught French before marrying WALTER BASS who formed his own investment company. They had six children who grew up during the depression; in the summers they would move to a two story log house on Kanis Road, where a large garden helped feed the family. Not only did the canned vegetables tide them over the winter, but each summer MILDRED BASS would can 365 jars of jam and jelly made from the blackberries, huckleberries, wild plums, and muscadines, that the children picked from the surrounding woods. Like her mother, Mildred was a member of the Mount Holly Board.

Another member of this family was GERTRUDE WATKINS, a sister of Annie. Gertrude was a lively tomboy who accompanied her father on the medical calls that he made in his pony cart. After high school in Little Rock she went to New York City where she became head of the (now called) Human Resources Department of Lord and Taylor. She was an active suffragist who led a parade in Little Rock, wearing white and helping to carry the banner that said: "Votes for Women."

Mildred's Oyster Mushroom Pie

Drain 12 ozs. fresh oysters, and to the liquor add whole milk or half and half to make 1 1/2 cups. Slice 2 cups fresh mushrooms. In a heavy saucepan sauté 1/2 stick of butter with 1/4 cup chopped green onions, 2 Tbs. finely chopped green pepper, 2 Tbs. chopped celery, and the mushrooms. Blend in 3 Tbs. flour. Stir in the measured liquid and cook, stirring until thickened. Season with a small amount of salt and freshly ground pepper. Add the oysters and turn into a shallow one quart buttered casserole. Top with either oyster crackers or cracker crumbs, or a pie crust made with 1 cup flour, 3 Tbs. butter, 2 Tbs. very cold water, rolled out to cover the casserole. Cut slits in top. Bake at 375 – 400 degrees for 40 minutes or until the crust is golden brown.

Pioneer television producer and personality for KTHV, EVELYN ELMEN created and produced the original noontime TV show, Eye on Arkansas. In 1965 she worked for Governor Winthrop Rockefeller; and then in the 70's and 80's she owned a company, Professional Medical Resources, which recruited nurses from Great Britain to work in Arkansas hospitals.

Evelyn loved to entertain. When friends would come over, a simple but outstanding meal was always in order. This is an easy meal to prepare for a crowd of hungry guests.

Evelyn's Shrimp

2 pounds shrimp, 16-20 peeled and deveined	1/2 stick butter
	1/3 cup olive oil
3 cloves garlic, minced	2 medium sized tomatoes, chopped
1 8-ounce box of mushrooms, sliced	1/2 cup dry white wine
2 Tbs. of capers, drained	2 tsp. fresh lemon juice
1 1/2 tsp. salt	1 tsp. pepper
3 cups cooked rice	

Melt butter and olive oil over medium heat in warm skillet. Once melted, add tomatoes, mushrooms and garlic. Cook for 10 minutes, making sure garlic does not brown. Add the wine, bring to gentle boil, and reduce volume in half, (about 10 minutes) on medium high. Add the olive oil and shrimp. Stir, and as soon as the shrimp turn pink (about 4 minutes), they are done. Sprinkle in salt and pepper. Add the capers and the lemon juice just before serving.

Ladle shrimp and sauce on rice to serve 4 people. A green salad and crusty French bread complete the meal.

Garlic Shrimp and Wild Rice

12 (1 pound) shrimp, deveined

Black pepper

2 to 3 stalks celery

1 ½ tsp. minced garlic

Oregano

1 box long grain wild rice

1 can chicken broth

3 Tbs. Italian dressing

Sprinkle shrimp with oregano and pepper. Start rice using chicken broth instead of water. DO NOT USE ANY BUTTER. Add shrimp 10 or 15 minutes before rice finishes cooking. After rice is cooked, add celery, minced garlic, and Italian dressing to taste. Serves 4.

Marjem Gill says this is one of her family's favorites.

Shrimp and Rice Casserole

(Can prepare day ahead. Pour cream around just before baking.)

1 stick plus 2 Tbs. butter

½ cup chopped green pepper

½ lb. fresh mushrooms

1 tsp. thyme

½ tsp. pepper

¼ tsp. Tabasco

1 Tbs. chopped pimento

3 lbs. peeled and de-veined shrimp

1 cup chopped yellow onion

2 packages (6 oz.) Uncle Ben's long grain wild rice

1 tsp. salt

2 tsp. Worcestershire sauce

1 Tbs. chopped chives

½ cup heavy cream or half-and-half

½ cup dry bread crumbs mixed with 3 Tbs. melted butter

Cook rice according to directions. Melt butter in skillet and sauté green pepper, onion, shrimp, and mushrooms 3 to 5 minutes, stirring constantly. Add thyme, etc. Mix over low heat. Fold in chives, pimento, and rice. Put in 3-quart greased casserole. Sprinkle bread crumb mixture on top of casserole. Pour cream around edges before baking. Bake at 375 degrees, uncovered, 35-40 minutes.

Seafood Casserole

4 slices of bread

$^{1}/_{2}$ medium green pepper

$^{1}/_{2}$ cup celery

1 or 2 cans crabmeat with juice

$^{1}/_{2}$ cup mayonnaise

1 egg

1 cup water

$^{1}/_{2}$ medium onion

$^{1}/_{2}$ lb. grated sharp cheese

1 - 2 cans shrimp, drained

1 - 2 drops of Tabasco sauce

Soak bread in water. Add cheese. Brown vegetables in butter until soft and add to bread and cheese mixture. Beat in egg and fold in mayonnaise with Tabasco sauce. Add crab and shrimp (may use fresh or frozen). Bake in greased casserole for 20 to 25 minutes at 325 degrees until firm and thoroughly heated. Serve with rice and a salad or green vegetable. It is delicious and should serve 6 to 8.

(This recipe was tested with Kroger Recipe Beginnings Mirepoix Cajun Blend for the pepper, onion, celery mix, Kraft finely shredded sharp cheddar for the cheese, medium shrimp, and Hellman's Light Mayonnaise. The vegetables were sautéed in a generous Tbs. of butter, and the casserole was sprayed with butter Pam. Use 2 cans of crabmeat and shrimp unless halving recipe.)

Vegetables & Side Dishes

⤙◦❦ TRUE GRITS ❦◦⤚

"True grits" is the apt description used by a northerner to describe southern ladies who pitched in to save the day when times were hard. Some opened their homes as boarding houses—with linen tablecloths and flowers on the tables; some sold the produce from their farms or their homemade jams and jellies; others risked public disapproval to save the public schools; and during the Civil War they managed farms as well as families when the war was at their doorsteps. During the great depression they used their varied talents to help out. You will encounter many "True Grit" women throughout this book.

Cheese Grits

1 ½ cups grits (regular)	5 cups water
1 lb. Old English or 1 pkg. Cracker Barrel sharp cheese	
2 Tbs. Worcestershire sauce	1 tsp. Tabasco
Dash of garlic powder	1 beaten egg, added last
Paprika to color	

Cook grits according to package directions. Add cheese and other ingredients. Put in buttered casserole to bake. Oven: 300 degrees for 40 minutes.

"Kingdom Come" Garlic Grits

1 ½ cup of cooked grits

While grits are hot, add ½ stick butter, 1 stick (6 oz.) garlic cheese* that has been cut into small pieces, and pour into buttered casserole dish. Cook 40 minutes at 300 degrees. Last 10 minutes, top with grated Sharp Cheddar and continue baking.

*Substitute for now defunct Kraft Garlic Cheese roll:

1 ½ lbs. American cheese grated (not "cheese food" not "cheese product," but REAL American cheese. You really need to get it from the deli counter of a good grocery store.)

½ lb. Velveeta – grated	3 oz. cream cheese – softened
1 tsp. seasoned salt	1 Tbs. garlic powder

Soften cheese and mix all ingredients together. Shape into four rolls, wrap separately in plastic wrap and store in ziplock bag in freezer. This cheese roll will give it the garlic cheese taste, but the color is not as orange.

The favorite dish of GEORGE ALEXANDER at his duck club, "Kingdom Come" near Stuttgart, was what came to be known as "Kingdom Come" Garlic Grits. Peter Booth, the duck club cook, was known for his great soul food, wild game dishes, and hush puppies. Hunting was put on the second burner as the guests enjoyed Kingdom Come's fabulous food created by this gifted chef.

LORENZO P. GIBSON and CAROLINE THOMAS GIBSON arrived in the territory of Arkansas in 1834 when Little Rock was little more than a crude village with mostly log cabins. They alternated residences between Little Rock and Rockport, where Lorenzo had built a country home called Ashwood on the banks of the Ouachita River. It was at this country home that Lorenzo bred and raised thoroughbred racehorses. A private racetrack was maintained for the training of young horses and for the entertainment of guests, who were frequent and many. Nearly everything for the family (ten children), and everything for the stock was raised on this place. Smokehouses were always filled with cured meats; and game was so abundant, often choice cuts of bear and venison were cured with the hams and bacon.

In 1849 they moved permanently to Little Rock. Their Little Rock home at 2215 Center Street was just as gracious as Ashwood. Outside was a large yard and garden. Poppies, daffodils, Persian cabbages, tuberoses, and old fashioned flowers bordered the walks.

Lorenzo was a man of many talents. He was a physician, an attorney, a farmer, a businessman, and a politician. He served in the Arkansas Legislature, lost a race for governor and was appointed Surveyor General of Arkansas by President Zachary Taylor. He was known for his moral and physical courage in refusing to carry arms when he was running for public office. This was equivalent to risking one's life in those days. He died in 1866 while running for U. S. Senator. Caroline died eight years later.

Corn Custard

2 cups fresh corn kernels	1/4 cup flour
1 tsp. sugar	1 tsp. salt
1/2 tsp. pepper	3 beaten eggs
2 cups milk	2 Tbs. butter or lard, melted

Mix corn with dry ingredients. Add eggs, milk, and butter. Bake in greased dish for about an hour (until a knife inserted into the center comes out clean). If oven is very hot, set dish in pan of hot water to cook.

Corn Oysters

2 cups grated green (fresh) corn	1 cup flour
1 egg	1 tsp. salt

Beat egg. Add flour, salt, and corn. If too dry, add milk. Drop spoonfuls of this mixture into hot deep fat. Fry 3-4 minutes until brown. Drain and serve.

DR. A. L. BREYSACHER cut quite a figure in his Prince Albert coat and silk top hat. Carrying a gold handled cane, he was the ideal example of a cultured, elegant gentleman. And, as his friends said about him, "when it came to hitting the spittoon, he was an excellent shot." He now resides at Mount Holly.

Interestingly, he served in both the Union and Confederate armies. He spent a year in the "far west" border at Camp Alert, Kansas, with the U. S. Army. After his return to St. Louis, he joined the Confederacy and was a surgeon for the duration of his service. He was a strong advocate for locating a medical school in Little Rock and was one of the founders of the Arkansas Medical School, where he served as a professor of obstetrics. Dr. Breysacher belonged to the Gilt Edge Hunting and Fishing Club. His main claim to fame, however, is that he delivered the infant Douglas MacArthur.

Polenta

Make mush (corn meal boiled in salt water, slowly, until thick) and turn into a square pan. When cold, cut in thin slices and lay in a baking dish; grate cheese over the mush, and dot with butter. Repeat layers, letting layer of cheese and butter be on top. Bake in moderate oven until cheese is thoroughly melted.

CAPTAIN THOMAS DARRAGH came to Little Rock in 1878 and was married three times. He was a riverboat captain for a number of years on the Mississippi and Arkansas rivers. He was a Mason, a member of Knights Templar, and later in life a manufacturer of shingles. His grandsons enjoy telling of his care of and interest in money. He used to brag that his investments earned interest even on the weekends.

Copper Pennies

2 lbs. carrots, scraped and sliced thin

1 cup sugar

1/4 cup vinegar

2 medium onions, sliced thin

1 can condensed tomato soup

1/2 cup vegetable oil

1 tsp. Worcestershire Sauce

Dash Tabasco

Boil carrots in salt water until tender and drain. Pour mixture over carrots and marinate overnight in refrigerator. Will keep 3 weeks.

Mildred Conway's Scalloped Oysters

(Rich side dish)

4 jars (10 oz.) of oysters, drained

1 bunch of parsley, washed,

    drained and chopped

Tony Cachere's Creole Seasoning

$^1/_2$ stick of butter

$1^1/_2$ tubes of Ritz crackers, crumbled

Lea & Perrin Worcestershire Sauce

In a 9" x 9" square buttered Pyrex dish, (1) layer $^1/_2$ of the oysters, (2) layer $^1/_2$ of crumbled Ritz crackers, (3) layer $^1/_2$ of chopped parsley, dot with butter, sprinkle with Creole seasoning and Worcestershire sauce, then repeat layers. (Do not try more than 2 layers, as they won't get done.) Bake in oven at 350 degrees for 25-30 minutes, until bubbly throughout, and slightly brown on top.

MILDRED HOLLIS CONWAY was a talented, beautiful, caring, creative person who made everything look so easy that her three daughters didn't realize how hard it was—for example, to arrange flowers, make a dress, prepare food, and entertain friends. On rainy days, she turned her dining room table into a ping-pong table for the girls.

CURRAN CONWAY had many interests, and his influence covered a wide range of civic, social, and church affairs in which he worked for more than 40 years. In 1917 he became a director of the Little Rock Boys Club and served for 47 years, earning him the name "Mr. Boys Club." He loved children and often told them that there was a town in Arkansas named for him. The obvious answer was Conway, but he said, "No, it's Bald Knob." He was completely bald.

AUGUSTUS HILL GARLAND was born in June, 1832, in Tipton county, Tennessee. He was an attorney who married SARAH VIRGINIA SANDERS with whom he had nine children. Four survived to adulthood. They moved to Little Rock in 1856, where he became one of the state's most prominent attorneys. In late 1860 he was admitted to the bar of the Supreme Court of the United States.

Garland opposed secession and reluctantly chose to support it after President Lincoln issued his call to arms. During the Civil War he served in the Confederate Congress in Richmond, Virginia. He returned to Arkansas in February 1865 to help facilitate the return of the state to the Union.

At that time he was pardoned by President Johnson and re-established his law practice. He presented his most significant case, Ex parte Garland, in 1865, arguing to allow former members of the Confederate government and military to argue cases before the court. He won and then hoped he could use the judicial system to prevent implementation of the Reconstruction Act that had passed Congress. The court declined to hear the case, so he turned to the political arena in his efforts to resist Reconstruction. When Arkansas was re-admitted to the Union, Garland was denied his previous seat in the U. S. Senate; so he returned to building his law practice.

Garland led the Democratic Party's successful effort toward ratification of the constitution and was elected governor. As the eleventh governor of Arkansas, he faced a number of problems, the largest being a state debt of around $17 million. With help from a board of finance he reduced the debt significantly over the next two years. He worked to improve Arkansas's image; and being a strong supporter of education, he urged the legislature to establish schools for the blind and deaf, actively participated in the search for a new president for the Arkansas Industrial University (now the U. of A., Fayetteville), and helped establish Branch Normal College (now UAPB) to make education more accessible to the African-American population of eastern Arkansas.

In 1877 Garland was again elected to the U. S. Senate and served on the Judiciary Committee. He worked to bring about tariff reform, regulation of interstate commerce, a federal prison system, federal aid to education, and civil service reform.

In 1885 he resigned from the Senate to accept the position of U. S. Attorney General in President Grover Cleveland's administration—the first cabinet-level Arkansan. He gave opinions on a wide range of topics including the purchase of silver under the Bland-Allison Act, the regulation of interstate commerce, and the process for granting public lands to railroads.

Garland retired from politics in 1888 but continued to live in Washington, D.C. and resumed his legal practice before the Supreme Court. He wrote several books, including Third Term Presidential (1896), Experience in the Supreme Court of the United States (1898), and A Treatise on the Constitution & Jurisdiction of the U.S. Courts (1898).

In January of 1899, while arguing a case before the Supreme Court, Garland suffered a stroke and died a few hours later. His body was returned to Arkansas and buried at Mount Holly. His grave is marked with a large granite obelisk, purchased through a public subscription drive, including pennies from school children all over the state. Garland County is named for him.

Cheese Pudding — "Soufflé"

14-16 slices of white bread,
    crusts trimmed
4 large eggs
Salt and pepper to taste

Softened butter
1 lb. sharp cheddar cheese shredded
3 cups milk

Butter 9" x 13" baking dish. Butter bread on one side, place butter side up in baking dish. Fit bread firmly and cover with half the cheese. Repeat the two layers. Beat eggs, add milk and seasonings. Pour carefully over mixture in dish. Be sure top layer is soaked. Let it set at least 2 hours or over night in the refrigerator. Bake at 375 degrees about one hour, until set. Serve at once. Serves 10 – 12.

A Wassell family recipe.

LAMARTINE BASCOM LEIGH recalled many years later that his first meal in Arkansas consisted of "crackling bread and bear meat." In spite of the cuisine, he stayed; founded the state's largest insurance agency; was active in civic affairs of Little Rock; and survived the only war fought entirely within the state's borders.

L. B. Leigh arrived in Little Rock in February of 1872. The November election of that year was called a "masterpiece of confusion." Promising to be "conservative, honest, just, and upright," Elisha Baxter took office as governor in January, 1873. Rev. Joseph Brooks, a former Iowa Methodist minister with a "voice like a brindle tail bull," protested the outcome. A year and three months later, in Brooks vs. Baxter, the judge declared in favor of Brooks as governor—without informing Baxter or his attorney.

Baxter was in his office in the state house when Brooks appeared "with an armed force of a dozen or twenty" and ejected him. The Brooks forces moved into the state house and increased their supplies of guns and ammunition by importing them straight to their offices in boxes marked "whiskey" and "Arkansas Reports." Little Rock became a battleground with Main Street as the battle line. Both sides bombarded President Grant asking for support, but Grant refused to interfere, saying the matter belonged to the state courts. However, federal troops did "wait on street corners to prevent bloodshed."

The Baxter forces cleaned and prepared for use an old cannon that had been spiked by the Confederate Army during the Civil War. Other cannons were set up on the front and back lawns of the capitol. The Baxter forces took control of the telegraph office; the mayor ordered all saloons closed; the postmaster refused to deliver mail addressed to the governor to either party; the windows of the capitol were barricaded with furniture; and the newspapers entered the fray with the *Gazette* saying Joseph Brooks should be dislodged even if the statehouse had to be demolished to do so, and calling President Grant a joker for saying that the courts must settle the contest.

The most famous fight of the war occurred when the Hallie, a steamboat filled with 28 Baxter volunteers, started upstream past the besieged state house. Despite the fact that the stern of the boat was barricaded with cotton bales the Brooks forces, firing from the banks of the river with rifles, were able to disable the boat and kill several people on board, including the Captain, Sam Houston. The newly arrived L. B. Leigh was shot in the leg and walked with a limp forever afterwards. People would often mention that Mr. Leigh had been injured in "the war." However, he lived a long life and was buried at Mount Holly in 1933.

The incident was the only "naval engagement" ever fought in Arkansas waters west of Little Rock. Although it only lasted twenty minutes, the "Hallie Rifles" were famous for many years. The war ended when President Grant ordered Brooks to disband his forces, declared Baxter as governor, and appointed Brooks as postmaster.

South Carolina Tomato Pie

2 Pillsbury pie crusts	1 ½ cups mayonnaise
2 cups shredded cheddar cheese	2 or 3 sliced tomatoes
Pieces of basil	

Put one pie crust in pan. Mix cheese and mayonnaise. Layer tomatoes, then cheese mixture, some basil ... more tomato, cheese, etc. until pan is filled. Put 2nd pie curst on top and cut a few air holes in it. Bake at 350 degrees until golden brown.

GOVERNOR GEORGE IZARD was born in England and was living in South Carolina when he was appointed the second Governor of the Territory of Arkansas in 1824 upon the resignation of Governor Miller. (Izard's father, Ralph, was in the first Congress and escorted George Washington to his inaugural.)

Izard, who pronounced his name with the accent on the second syllable, had been a military man. He had taken part in the war of 1812, and tried to organize a militia to protect the citizens here from the Indians.

He was a profound scholar—literate in Latin, French, and Spanish. He had been in excellent health, but had a premonition that he was about to die. So he had a casket made, had his grave dug and walled in brick, and died about a month later. His extensive library sank on its way back to South Carolina. Izard County is named for him.

Living in Arkansas was pretty primitive in the early 1820's. It is said that living quarters were mere shacks and that the food consisted of bread, meat and coffee. There were no women here at first; when they arrived, things began to improve.

Hoppin' John

1 package (1 pound) black-eyed peas

½ lb. sliced salt pork or bacon

½ tsp. salt

2 cloves garlic, crushed

1 large green pepper, chopped fine

1 ½ cups boiling water

3 pints cold water

1 tsp. Tabasco sauce

2 Tbs. bacon fat

2 medium onions, chopped

1 ½ cups uncooked long grain rice

1 can (16 oz.) whole tomatoes, undrained

Cover peas with water in large kettle. Soak overnight. Add pork, Tabasco, and salt. Cover and cook over low heat about 30 minutes. While peas are cooking, sauté onions and green pepper in bacon fat until tender. Add garlic, rice, tomatoes, and boiling water. Cook until rice is tender and water is absorbed, about 20 to 25 minutes, stirring occasionally. Combine mixtures. Makes 8 cups.

Hoppin' John #2

2 cups shelled black-eyed peas (or 2 pkgs, 10 ozs. each, frozen black-eyed peas)

2 (¼" thick) slices salt pork

2 cups hot cooked rice

½ to 1 tsp. salt

(depending on saltiness of the salt pork)

1 cup boiling water

2 Tbs. butter

¼ tsp. pepper

Cook the black-eyed peas with the salt pork in boiling water in covered saucepan 30 – 40 minutes until peas are tender. Fork in the rice, butter, salt, and pepper and heat over lowest heat about 5 minutes to drive off excess steam. Fluff up with a fork and serve. Serves 4 to 6.

Mushroom Pastry

1 lb. mushrooms, sliced

2 medium onions, chopped

$^1/_2$ cup light cream

1 tsp. thyme

Piecrust dough for double – crust 8" pie

$^1/_3$ cup butter

$^1/_3$ cup flour

1 $^1/_2$ Tbs. sweet sherry

Salt and pepper to taste

Trim and slice mushrooms. In a skillet melt the butter and sauté the onions until transparent. Add mushrooms and sauté until lightly golden. Sprinkle flour in the pan and gently stir until blended and golden but not brown. Remove from heat and slowly add cream, sherry, and thyme, stirring until smooth. Replace on the heat and cook until thickened. Season with salt and pepper. Allow to cool. This can be refrigerated overnight.

Roll out piecrust and fill it with cooled mushroom filling. Cover with latticed strips of crust. Preheat oven to 450 degrees and bake 20 minutes. Serves 8.

DR. JAMES H. LENOW was a charter member of the Arkansas Medical Society and was instrumental in establishing the University of Arkansas Medical School in what is now McArthur Park. (There is a plaque there.) He served as its first dean. Dr. Lenow was also the Arkansas State Penitentiary physician; and he performed the first human dissection in Arkansas in 1874.

Caroline Walton's Scalloped Mushrooms

Peel the mushrooms and break into pieces. Saute in hot butter 3 or 4 minutes. To 2 cups of mushrooms add 3 Tbs. of flour and $1/2$ tsp. chopped parsley. Stir and cook until the flour has become absorbed by the butter. Then add 1 cup of stock, cream, or milk. Stir until the sauce boils, then simmer gently for 10 minutes. Add 1 tsp. lemon juice, a dash of paprika, and $1/4$ tsp. of salt. Remove from fire. Beat the yolk of 1 egg with 2 Tbs. of milk or cream and stir into the mixture. Fill buttered shells or baking dish with the preparation. Stir 1 cup of cracker crumbs into $1/3$ cup of melted butter and spread on top of the preparation. Let the dish stand in the oven long enough to brown the crumbs. Canned mushrooms can be used.

S—Que—Wi (Cherokee Cabbage)

1 small cabbage, cut into bite-sized chunks
1 small green pepper, cut in small, thin strips
$1/8$ tsp. pepper

3 Tbs. bacon or pork drippings
1 tsp. salt

Fry the cabbage in the bacon or pork drippings in a large, heavy kettle over moderately high heat just until cabbage begins to wilt and brown slightly—8 to 10 minutes. Add the green pepper and continue to fry and stir until the raw green color goes out of the pepper. Clap the lid on the kettle, turn the heat down low, and let cabbage "wilt" 10 to 15 minutes It should be nicely glazed with the meat drippings, touched with brown here and there, but still somewhat crisp. Add salt and pepper, toss well to mix, and serve. Makes 4 to 6 servings.

(This is great. Even the kids like it! You can use peppered bacon, also red cabbage with the green cabbage.)

~∞♦ THE TRAIL OF TEARS ♦∞~

The Trail of Tears is rightly remembered as a grave injustice to and a tragic time for the Native American population of the United States. QUATIE ROSS (Nee Elizabeth Hensley)—the wife of John Ross, who was chief of the Cherokees—was one of those martyrs along the "trail where they cried." Her name was Elizabeth, but she changed it to Quatie, the Cherokee equivalent of Betty or Betsy, when she married Ross. They were prominent, well-to-do people in Tennessee before they were forced to leave for the Indian Territory (Oklahoma). Theirs was the last group to take part in the Trail of Tears, and they traveled on the large boat that they owned, the Victoria. They were traveling on the Arkansas River in bitter cold with snow and sleet. One of the children aboard became sick, so Quatie gave the child her blanket. She herself developed pneumonia and died February 1, 1839, when they were near Little Rock. (The child lived.) Quatie was buried in the Old Cemetery, and the boat went on.

Chester Ashley, William E. Woodruff, and some other city leaders had a small stone erected in her memory because of her position as wife of the Chief. She was later moved to Mount Holly in the Albert Pike lot. The original stone was found—broken but still readable. Because of the gradual deterioration of the stone in its exposed

position at Mount Holly, the cemetery board voted to give the original marker to the Historic Arkansas Museum. A Quatie Ross marker remains at Mount Holly, though. The General George Izard Chapter of the United States Daughters of 1812 erected a stone memorializing her on the Albert Pike lot in 1936; and a footstone was placed on the site by the Continental Society of Daughters of the Indian Wars.

When American Indians visit graves, they always leave something to show that they have been there: rocks, feathers, jewelry, coins, etc. For a long time there were a large crystal, a small piece of petrified wood, quarters, dimes, nickels, and pennies. Sadly, the crystal and wood have disappeared, along with quarters; but a lot of pennies, rocks and a few dimes still remain along with additional items frequently added.

Corn Pones

A Cherokee staple. If fried in a skillet, the bread becomes Corn Pone; if baked in hot coals, Ash Cake. These are heavy breads, but the Cherokees would have them no other way. Great used to sop up the "pot likker" of boiled turnip greens, etc. Makes 6 servings.

1 $^1/_2$ cups corn meal (preferably stone-ground white meal)

1 $^1/_2$ tsp. baking powder $^1/_2$ tsp. salt

3 Tbs. bacon drippings $^3/_4$ cup cold water

Stir together the corn meal, baking powder, and salt in a medium-size mixing bowl. Briskly mix in the bacon drippings and water and stir just enough to make a stiff dough. Shape the dough into 6 round, flat cakes about $^1/_2$ inch thick. Heat about 2 Tbs. bacon drippings or lard in a very large, heavy, iron skillet just until it begins to smoke. Add the pones, reduce heat slightly, and brown well—about 10 minutes on each side. The pones will be crisp and brown outside, chewy inside.

Candied Squash

(In a roasting pan or Dutch oven)

Cut Hubbard squash* in 3" to 4" squares and lay the first ones rind down, next layer rinds up. Combine and pour over squash:

1 cup water $^1/_2$ cup melted shortening

1 cup white or brown sugar

Cover and cook until tender (45 minutes at 350 degrees.)

*A variety of winter squash having a green or yellow skin and yellow flesh.

B. FRANK MACKEY, a former police officer, served on the Little Rock School Board (1959-1963) during the period of transition to compliance with the federal court orders to desegregate. He worked to re-open the Little Rock public high schools, closed during the '58-'59 school year by then Governor Orval E. Faubus. He was elected Pulaski County Sheriff in 1962 and served three terms. In 1968 he was elected County Judge and served until he retired from public office in 1976.

Grant County Cornbread Stuffing

2 cups cornbread crumbs

1 cup celery, cut in small pieces

$^1\!/_2$ stick butter

$^1\!/_2$ tsp. pepper

1 egg plus enough warm broth to make a soft mixture

4 cups stale white bread crumbs

$^1\!/_2$ cup onions, cut fine

1 tsp. salt

1 $^1\!/_2$ tsp. poultry seasoning or ground sage

Cook celery and onions in butter until soft but not overdone.

Mix all together. If you make it up and let it sit an hour before baking the seasoning blends better. Bake at 350 degrees in a buttered casserole. *MRS. B. FRANK MACKEY*

Elizabeth Leigh Vaughan's Potato Salad

18 medium potatoes (#5 bag), peeled   6 eggs, hard boiled and chopped

3 heads of celery – only the best part, trimmed and diced

Dried onion to taste   Salt, onion salt, pepper, and paprika

DRESSING: MIX TOGETHER

Mayonnaise (either Kraft or Hellmann's, but not sweet)

A little milk   Very fresh sour cream

Boil dried onion in bouillon for about 10 minutes or until softened. Add potatoes and cook until done, but firm. Drain, cool and cube. Add eggs and toss with dressing. Season to taste with a little onion salt and paprika. Serve room temperature or chilled. Garnish with celery leaves. Better the next day.

Wild Rice

(In the past wild rice was a great delicacy and hard to find in the stores. It would also arrive still containing some grit from harvesting. If you suspect this is so, take a strainer and rinse the rice in cold water 2-3 times.)

Follow cooking directions to simmer rice 50-60 minutes in a combination of water and chicken broth. If using bouillon cube, be careful not to get it too salty. Rice is done when still a bit firm to taste and about a quarter of the grains are open.

Season with butter and sliced mushrooms and/or chopped pecans that have been browned in butter in a hot skillet. (Option: a little Adolph's is wonderful!)

ELIZABETH LEIGH VAUGHAN graduated in 1932 from Vassar College and attended Union Theological Seminary in New York. She was a founding member of the Bronxville Junior League. The popular song, "Betty Co-Ed," was written by Paul Fogarty and sung by Rudy Vallee. It was arranged by Frank E. Barry and copyrighted in 1930. It hit #4 on the "charts" in that year. It is believed to have been inspired by Elizabeth Leigh, wife of THOMAS R. VAUGHAN. The Vaughans now reside at Mount Holly.

A civic activist, CATHERINE RIGHTSELL RICE was the granddaughter of R. J. Rightsell, the first superintendent of the Little Rock Public School District and great-granddaughter of Judge WILLIAM WALLACE WILSHIRE, former Arkansas Supreme Court Chief Justice and U. S. Congressman. She was chairman of the fundraising drive sponsored by the Diabetes Association that provided the first heart and lung machine installed at UAMS.

Green Rice

1 cup brown rice	2 $\frac{1}{2}$ cups water
1 tsp. butter	Cook for $\frac{1}{2}$ hour until liquid is absorbed.

Grate 2 cups cheese and 1 onion.

ADD: 2 cups milk $\qquad$ $\frac{1}{2}$ cup butter, melted

1 cup chopped parsley $\qquad$ 2 beaten eggs

Mix cheese and onion mixture with rice. Bake slowly 1 $\frac{1}{2}$ hours in large buttered casserole.

Lemon Rice

¹/₄ lb. stick of butter or **4** Tbs. ghee

1 tsp. salt

1 tsp. black mustard seed (yellow will do)

2 tsps. turmeric

3 cups cooked rice

Juice of 1 lemon, strained

Melt the butter or ghee. Add the seasonings to it, and stir well until the seasonings blend and the mustard seeds dance. Then add the rice. Stir well until all heats through, then add the lemon juice.

The rice, elegantly golden, delicately spiced, is ideal to serve with simple curries—or with many Western dishes, for that matter.

Green Chili Rice

1 cup long grain rice

1 pint sour cream

1 can (7oz.) green chilies, diced

³/₄ lb. Monterey Jack Cheese, grated

Salt & pepper to taste

Cook rice. Mix cooked rice, sour cream, green chilies, salt and pepper together. Butter casserole and layer rice mixture, then layer of cheese, another layer of rice, topped with cheese. Bake 350 degrees for 30 minutes. Best made a day ahead!

GEORGE B. ROSE was born in Batesville in 1860, the son of U. M. Rose, a distinguished lawyer whose statue stands in the national capitol. The family moved to Little Rock in 1865 and George became a partner in his father's law firm—one of the oldest west of the Mississippi River.

MARION KIMBALL ROSE (Mrs. George B.) was born in Salem, Massachusetts although she would not say when. The family came to Little Rock in 1874, where her father was also a well-respected lawyer. With her husband, she attended the second Peace Conference at the Hague in 1907. Her father-in-law was a delegate with the rank of ambassador. She was also presented to King George V and Queen Mary when the American Bar Association met in London in 1924.

Marion was a member of the Aesthetic Club and First Presbyterian Church. She considered herself the social arbiter of the city; and Mrs. Hanger, social writer for the *Arkansas Gazette*, considered herself that, too. It was the custom for the social writer to describe the dresses of prominent ladies at functions, and one time Mrs. Hanger neglected to describe Mrs. Rose's dress—brought back from Europe—and she complained. Thereafter, Mrs. Hanger wrote up the *same* dress on every occasion.

Eggplant Supreme

Scoop out flesh from large eggplant, save skin

$^1/_2$ stick butter	1 small yellow onion
3 ribs celery	1 green pepper
2 tsp. basil	$^1/_2$ tsp. sage
Salt and pepper to taste	4 green onions, green and white parts
2 eggs beaten	1 cup Monterey Jack cheese, grated
1 $^1/_2$ cups seasoned bread crumbs	

Boil eggplant, cut in chunks, drain. Sauté onions. Add other ingredients, except bread crumbs. Top with bread crumbs. Bake at 350 degrees for 30 minutes. Re-fit in the eggplant skin to serve.

Mrs. Rose entertained a lot; and at one small dinner she served eggplant that had been scooped out, flavored and returned to the shell—a new way to serve it at the time. However, when it was offered to another formidable lady first, it is said that she took the whole thing.

Old Fashioned Boston Baked Beans

1 lb. white beans (dry or canned)

1/4 cup molasses

1 Tbs. packed brown sugar

1 tsp. salt

1/4 tsp. black pepper or red pepper flakes

2 medium onions, sliced

2 Tbs. tomato paste or 1/2 cup ketchup

1 Tbs. vinegar

1/2 tsp. dry mustard

4 cups hot water

Rinse beans, discarding any discolored ones. In a large saucepan, soak beans overnight or quick soak (see below) and drain. Add water to cover by at least 2 inches, bring to a boil and simmer for 30 minutes. Drain. (If using canned beans, simply rinse and drain.)

In bean pot or 8-cup casserole, spread onion slices. Mix molasses, tomato paste, sugar, vinegar, salt, mustard, and pepper. Pour over onions. Add drained beans and hot water.

Cover and bake in 250 degree oven for 6 hours. Uncover and bake for 1 hour longer, adding water as necessary to keep beans covered.

(Quick soaking: Place rinsed beans in large saucepan; cover with 2 inches of water and bring to a boil. Boil 10 minutes and drain. Cover with cold water; let soak 30 minutes and drain.)

If only the tale behind BENJAMIN SHATTUCK'S epitaph could easily be discerned. His tombstone tells us that he was born in Massachusetts in 1777," educated at Harvard University, served his country in her Navy, and then sought a home in the Great West." When Robert Crittenden was ordered by the U. S. Government in 1823 to appoint "a suitable person to survey the land to be appropriated to the Cherokee Indians in this territory, in exchange for the lands relinquished by them in the old nation east of the Mississippi," he chose Benjamin. But nothing tells us why a young man from a prominent New England family came to Little Rock in the early 1820s and why his tombstone says: "Endured with equanimity the trials of a checkered life until he met his Father and his God." He died in 1831 and is buried in the lot of his friends, the Woodruffs. This perhaps explains the last of his epitaph: "In gratitude to the neighbors and friends who soothed his dying pillow."

A stroll through Mount Holly will bring a smile to your face at some of the spelling. Accuracy was not always critical; and an interesting example is the tombstone of WILLIAM GILCHRIST, who was born in North Carolina in 1790, came to Arkansas in 1836, and died at his plantation home outside of Little Rock in 1843. Eight years later his Masonic lodge erected a granite monument 17 feet high to honor Gilchrist, the first Grand Master of Masons in Arkansas. Carved by the prominent stonemason Robert Brownlee, this enormous tombstone contains a quantity of elaborate Masonic emblems, but also the words "apeareth" and "vanesheth."

Carrot Loaf

6 ozs. unsalted butter   2 lbs. carrots, peeled and cut into $^1/_4$ inch slices

$^1/_4$ pound mushrooms, cut into $^1/_4$ inch slices

1 lb. fresh spinach, rinsed well and dried (baby spinach)

6 eggs   1 cup grated Gruyere or Swiss cheese (4 ozs.)

1 tsp. salt   1 tsp. freshly ground pepper

Melt 2 ozs. of the butter in a large skillet over medium heat. Add carrots and sauté slowly until tender, about 25 minutes. Chop coarsely and place in a bowl.

Increase heat to high and melt 1 oz. of the butter in the same skillet. Add the mushrooms and sauté for 2 minutes. Chop coarsely and add to carrots. Set aside.

Melt 2 ozs. butter over medium-high heat in the same skillet, add the spinach and sauté until wilted, about 2 minutes. Chop coarsely, place in a separate bowl and set aside.

Line an 8 $^1/_2$ by 4 $^1/_2$ by 2 $^1/_2$ inch loaf pan with aluminum foil. Butter foil with the remaining butter. Beat together 4 eggs, the cheese, salt and pepper in a medium bowl; add to the carrot mixture; and mix well. Add the remaining eggs (beaten) to the spinach and mix well. Spread half the carrot mixture over the bottom of the pan, cover with the spinach mixture, and top with the remaining carrot mixture. Cover with plastic wrap and refrigerate.

Preheat the oven to 400 degrees. Remove the plastic wrap, cover the loaf pan loosely with foil and place in a roasting pan. Add enough boiling water to come halfway up the sides of the loaf pan. Bake 1 hour or until a knife plunged in the center comes out clean. Uncover, invert the loaf onto a serving platter and remove foil. Slice and serve. 8 servings. (Good warmed the next day.)

Apricot Casserole

1 large can apricots. Drain and reserve liquid.

Spread butter on bottom of a casserole dish. Layer apricots, then dot butter on top, sprinkle with brown sugar, then layer of Ritz crackers. Repeat. Pour a little of reserved apricot juice over the top to moisten. Bake at 350 degrees until heated through.

Serves 10.

ANNE BOND

Ragoo French Beans

String and cut beans, boil them tender. Put a piece of butter worked in flour into your stew pan and fry a couple of sliced onions; then put in the beans, with a little nutmeg, pepper and salt. Beat the yolk of an egg with a little cream; stir into the bean mixture a minute or two, and send them to the table.

WILLIAM BOOKER WORTHEN was born in 1852, and MOLLIE PEAY WORTHEN was born in 1856. They were married in 1879. He was a banker all of his adult life and started his own bank in 1877 which lasted over one hundred years. He had a part in most of the developments in the city: water works, street paving and the likes. At the request of the Arkansas Bankers Association he wrote the book Early Banking in Arkansas, a definitive account of the checkered banking history in the state. He belonged to the Knights of Honor, Royal Arcanum, the N. L. Hunting and Fishing Club, and was an officer in the "Hallie Rifles," which took part in the Brooks-Baxter War on the Baxter side.

Worthen Bank moved into its new building at 4th and Main in 1929. Hoover was president and Parnell was governor. Mrs. Worthen's finest hour came in 1933 when the new president, Roosevelt, closed all the banks for a "bank holiday." Mollie and her son George put their combined fortune of $250,000 with $50,000 from all the rest of the Worthen family, to make the required amount of $300,000 for preferred stock to back the common stock of the bank. As a result, Worthen Bank was the first bank to open in Greater Little Rock after the crash and could pay 100 cents on the dollar on all deposits. It was a big risk, but it paid off; Worthen grew from a small bank to the largest in the state in a few years. W. B. Worthen died in 1911, and Mollie Peay Worthen died in 1944.

When W. B. Worthen married Mollie Peay he accumulated a lot of in-laws. Many of them were happy to borrow money from his bank, but they were not as enthusiastic about repaying the loans. One of them said that Brother Booker was a hard man. When the tall obelisk was erected over his tomb one of the Peays remarked, "Well, that is as near heaven as Brother Booker will ever get."

Mrs. Booker Worthen's Parsley Soufflé

4 Tbs. butter   **4 Tbs.** flour

1 small onion, grated

BLEND IN BLENDER:

$^3/_4$ cup sharp cheese $^3/_4$ cup parsley

1 $^1/_3$ cup milk

Combine mixtures; cook, stirring constantly. Stir in 5 egg yolks till thickened. Cool. Fold in 5 egg whites, beaten. Bake at 375 degrees for about 30 minutes.

Serves 6 to 8.

Marinated Carrots

Scrape and cut 1 lb. carrots into strips. (Cut each carrot into 4 strips.) Marinate in 1 cup water, $^1/_4$ cup vinegar, 1 tsp. salt and $^1/_2$ tsp. garlic powder (or 2 or 3 mashed garlic cloves). Let stand several hours or overnight in the refrigerator. Drain.

Add 1 Tbs. each dried basil and oregano, or any other herb(s). Let stand for an hour or two for flavors to blend.

Mary Worthen

This monument on the Albert Pike lot was for their children. The cut-off columns indicate lives cut short.

Cakes

TOM FLETCHER was born in 1876, grew up at 10th and Izard streets with devout Christian (Campbellite) parents. On Sundays he went to Sunday school, then church, then home for lunch and back to church for evening prayer. If he wanted any diversion in the afternoon, he was allowed to walk through Mount Holly Cemetery, which was close by. No wonder he turned against organized religion. He graduated from Rose Polytechnic Institute in Terre Haute, Indiana, and moved to Fletcher Farm, six miles beyond Scott, in 1906.

Being off the main road, he became pretty much self-sufficient with his own cotton gin, acetylene gas for lights and Old River water piped into the house, which was finished in 1912. As river water was not drinkable, he built a cistern with rainwater from the roof cleansed through a charcoal filter.

After he was married, he faithfully drove his wife, Mamie, from their home at Scott, 20 miles away to her church, Trinity Episcopal Cathedral. Then after 25 years he officially joined it.

MAMIE SANDLIN FLETCHER was born in 1887 in Morrilton, and she and Tom were married in 1911. They had two children, Thomas, Jr. and Mary Sandlin—whom she home schooled until they entered high school. He went to Exeter and she went to Little Rock Senior High, later Central High.

There wasn't much to do in those days, and Mamie did not drive; so she gardened a lot, worked crossword puzzles (they were new then) and translated Latin for fun. They moved to Little Rock in 1948, and Tom died three weeks later. Mamie learned to drive, joined the Edelweiss Club and the Aesthetic Club (that accepted no member outside the city limits), and enjoyed being near her friends for her last years.

Mamie Fletcher's Pecan Cake

3 eggs	$3/4$ cup sugar	$1/2$ tsp. baking powder
1 cup ground pecans	$1/2$ tsp. vanilla	$1/2$ pint whipping cream

Separate eggs and beat yolks and whites separately. Add sugar to yolks and beat again, then fold in all other ingredients, except cream. Bake in 8" greased square pan lined with greased waxed paper or aluminum foil. Cook at 350 degrees about 20 minutes or until toothpick comes out clean. Cool. Peel away waxed paper, cut into two layers with a bread knife and spread whipped cream between layers and on top. Chill 3 hours or overnight.

Warren Tea Cakes

An "old, antique recipe for a delicious tea cake, very nice for tea and very wholesome"

Three (3) teacups of sugar

Three (3) chicken eggs

One half (1/2) of a teaspoonful of salt

Two (2) teaspoons of baking powder

Two (2) teaspoons of vanilla flavoring

One (1) teacup of fresh firm butter

One (1) teaspoonful of soda

Three quarter (3/4) cupful of buttermilk or sweet milk

Four and a half (4 1/2) teacups of sifted flour

Cream butter and sugar. Add the chicken eggs. (Check the eggs for soundness. Put the egg in water; if fresh the egg will sink to the bottom.) Mix very well. Add the flour, soda, salt, and baking powder together with the buttermilk or sweet milk. Add the vanilla flavoring. Work well together with a spoon. The batter must be as stiff as can be beaten with a spoon. One secret of having good tea cakes is to have the batter thin. Grease the flat tin tray on which you drop the batter.

Preheat the oven to 350 degrees and bake for about seven (7) to eight (8) minutes until the edges turn a light golden brown. This recipe makes a bunch of tea cakes. When you want them for tea in the Winter make them up in the cool of the morning. When you want them for tea in the Summer make them up in the evening directly after dinner. The tea cakes should be eaten fresh.

NATHAN WARREN, a free man of color in antebellum Little Rock, was famous for his baking and confections. His customers tried to get him to share his recipes, but he wouldn't because that was an important part of his business. In fact, his great-granddaughter Marion Johnson Fowler Armstrong has not been able to document any family recipes coming from Nathan Warren. Among Nathan Warren's most esteemed products were his tea cakes, and Judge Joyce Williams Warren and her husband James Medrick Warren are sharing their family tea cake recipe publicly for the first time. This might be as close as we can come to the original recipe. Enjoy.

Vaughan Family "Tea Cakes"

1 cup butter

2 eggs

1 tsp. vanilla

1 cup sugar

1 Tbs. water

1 tsp. baking powder

Enough flour to roll and cut: 5 to 7 cups

Cream butter and sugar. Mix in eggs. Mix water and vanilla and add. Sift baking powder with 1 to 2 cups of flour and stir into batter. Continue mixing in more flour until almost enough to roll. Chill 1 to 2 hours. Add rest of flour needed to roll cookies as thin as you can. Cut with a simple drinking glass. Bake on cookie sheets greased with a good salty butter. You will taste it later. Cool on a wire rack and store between layers of waxed paper in metal tins. This recipe can be doubled.

"Tea Cakes" is the old name for sugar cookies. This recipe is from the grandmother of THOMAS RAE VAUGHAN. These cookies are rich and are not meant to be frosted or eaten with other strong flavors. Indeed they taste best with tea, milk or Christmas eggnog.

Blueberry Cheesecake

PIE CRUST:

1 cup graham cracker crumbs (fresh, not "ready to use" kind. Crush.)

$^1/_2$ cup sugar $^1/_2$ stick of melted butter

Mix and form the pie crust in pie pan using the back of a spoon.

FILLING:

1 can blueberry pie filling   8 oz. Philadelphia cream cheese

$^1/_2$ cup sugar   2 large eggs

1 cup heavy cream, whipped with 1 tsp. sugar.

Combine cream cheese, sugar and one egg. Mix thoroughly and then add the other egg and mix again. Pour over pie crust and cook about 25 minutes at 325 degrees. Let cool. Pour over top, part of can of blueberry pie filling. Cover with whipped cream. Chill and serve. Simple to make and sinfully good.

Kentucky Bourbon Cake

1 pound butter	2 cups white sugar

2 cups light brown sugar, firmly packed (1 # box)

6 eggs	5 cups flour
1 tsp. salt	1 tsp. mace

2 cups good bourbon (Old Granddad or Virginia Gentleman)

3 cups or 1 lb. chopped fresh pecans

Cream butter, sugar, and eggs in mixer. Sift dry ingredients together. Add dry ingredients alternating with liquor in thirds. Add pecans. Fill a well-greased 10" tube pan. (Fills either one angel food cake pan or one spiral bundt pan and one smaller one.) Cake is done when toothpick comes out clean. Cool 15 minutes and remove to rack.

Tom Vaughan Jr. discovered this recipe when on his medical residency at Vanderbilt University. It became a family Christmas cake immediately. This cake enjoys pecans when they are fresh. Like many a Christmas cake it can be kept almost indefinitely if wrapped in aluminum foil and given an occasional "anointing" with additional bourbon. This is one that improves with age!

CHARLES PIERRE BERTRAND was born in Philadelphia in 1808. He came to Little Rock in early 1820, and was here so long that he was fondly known as "old settler." He learned printing as an apprentice to William E. Woodruff, finishing in 1829. He then started the state's second newspaper, the *Arkansas Advocate*, in opposition to the *Gazette*. He sold it in 1835 to Albert Pike. Charles was secretary of the state's first Constitutional Convention, and Little Rock mayor, 1855-56. He was a lawyer, director of the new Little Rock Gas Co., and president of Arkansas Telegraph. He died after a long illness in 1865.

Nothing Crumb Cake

1 1/2 cups firmly packed dark brown sugar

2 1/2 cups flour   1/2 cup butter

1 tsp. baking soda   1/2 tsp. salt

1/2 cup buttermilk   1 egg

Place sugar, flour and butter in a large bowl and rub together until fine and crumbly. Measure out half and reserve. Stir baking soda and salt into buttermilk and mix into half the crumbs. Beat in egg and pour batter into a well-greased 9" by 9" baking pan. Scatter remaining crumbs over the top. Bake in a moderate oven (350) for 40 to 45 minutes until crumb topping is tinged with brown. Let cool upright in its pan 10 minutes before cutting into squares and serving. A Pennsylvania Dutch recipe.

Masonic burials of interest include the death of JAMES A. HENRY, who lost his balance and fell down a stairway at the Masonic Lodge. His fellow Masons rushed to his assistance, but his skull was fractured and he died soon afterwards. The next night at midnight a Scottish Rite burial service was held at the Albert Pike Cathedral, "open to Masons of every degree and the public at large." According to the *Arkansas Gazette:* "The remains will be in state in the Scottish Rite cathedral from Wednesday midnight until Thursday afternoon, when the funeral will take place under escort and direction of the grand commandery, Knights Templar, who will conduct the final burial services at the grave ... then to Mount Holly cemetery where the remains will be deposited in solemn form."

White Funeral Cakes

(From an heirloom recipe written down in 1914)

6 cups cake flour, sifted twice	½ tsp. baking soda
1 cup (2 sticks) butter, at room temperature	
2 cups granulated sugar	2 tsps. grated nutmeg
1 Tbs. caraway seeds	1 cup milk

Sift two cups of the flour with the baking soda and set aside. Cream the butter and sugar together in a bowl. Add the nutmeg and caraway seeds. Add the milk alternately with the two cups of flour mixed with the seeds, stirring together gently. Gradually sift in the remaining flour and work it in, to form a soft dough. Cover and refrigerate at least two hours, preferably overnight.

Preheat oven to 325 degrees.

Roll dough one-quarter inch thick on a lightly floured board and cut into shapes about 3" in diameter. Place on an ungreased baking sheet. Bake about 20 minutes, until the cakes are firm and turning golden on the bottom. The scraps may be rerolled, cut and baked.

Hummingbird Cake

("John's Birthday Cake")

3 cups flour	2 cups sugar
1 tsp. baking soda	1 tsp. salt
1 tsp. cinnamon	3 eggs, beaten
1 1/2 tsp. vanilla	8 oz. un-drained crushed pineapple
1 cup chopped pecans	2 cups chopped bananas
1 cup vegetable oil	

Combine flour, sugar, soda, salt, and cinnamon in large mixing bowl; add eggs & oil, stirring until moistened. Do not beat. Stir in vanilla, pineapple, pecans, & bananas. Spoon batter into 3 greased and floured 9" round cake pans. Bake 25-30 minutes at 350 degrees or until toothpick inserted in center of cake comes out clean. Cool in pans 10 minutes, remove, and cool.

Don't use electric mixer! Hand beat only.

ICING:

1 lb. box of confectioner's sugar	1 8 oz. cream cheese
1/2 cup butter (1 stick)	1 tsp. vanilla

Cream butter & cheese until smooth. Add sugar & mix well, add vanilla. Top with nuts.

JEFF DAVIS, a Democrat and one of our more colorful politicians, was elected to three terms as governor and one as United States Senator. (He should not be confused with Jefferson Davis of Mississippi, who was president of the Confederate States of America.) Although he had very little formal education, he passed the local bar in Russellville at the age of nineteen and had the gift of oratory. His stories about backwoods humor had great appeal, especially for people in rural Arkansas who were in the majority at that time. He died suddenly in 1913.

(Cleo Davis, who married his grandson, also named Jeff, is the keeper of the family traditions and graciously gave us this recipe.)

Tedia's "Stained-Glass" Nut-Fruit Cake

OTELIA ALEXANDER's famous Christmas cake served at her home, Illallee.

3 cups of nuts (pecans, English walnuts & Brazil nuts)

1 lb. of pitted dates

1 cup of candied maraschino cherries, red and green

³/₄ cup sifted flour

¹/₂ tsp. baking powder

¹/₂ tsp. salt

³/₄ cup of sugar

Whip 4 eggs and mix into dry ingredients. Dredge fruit and nuts in mixture. Grease rectangular bread pans and line with brown paper. Grease well again. Cook 1 hour and 45 minutes at 300 degrees. Avoid over cooking.

Note: As soon as these cakes are done they should be removed and wrapped in white linen cloths with bourbon poured over. Let sit a day or so. To serve, slice very thin. This gives the stained-glass effect.

Aunt Hattie's White Fruit Cake

7 eggs	1 lb. butter
2 cups sugar	4 cups flour
1 lb. dates	1 lb. golden seedless raisins
3 pts. shelled pecans	1 cup bourbon

Cut dates in slices with shears, separate raisins from stems and pecans from any shells. If you can get pecans in broken lots, it will save time; if in halves, break them in two as you go. Put all this into bowl and set aside until needed. Cream butter and sugar until light and fluffy. Add to this the well-beaten eggs. Sift some flour over nuts and fruits, mixing well and separating the pieces of dates that stick together. Be sure that all pieces are coated with flour.

To the sugar, butter, and egg mixture, begin to add alternately the flour, nuts, fruits, and bourbon a little at a time. Stir well after each addition so that all fruits and nuts are well covered with the batter.

The yield is 7 pounds. If you wish one large cake, bake at 275 degrees for about 2 hours. If you make several small cakes – say 2 pounds or a little over – bake at 300 degrees for 45 minutes to an hour. Don't cook too long – when cake tester comes out clean, it is done.

Harriet Parker Powell was the great aunt of Mary Fordyce Allsopp; and her husband was a descendant of AUGUSTUS WINFIELD after whom Winfield Methodist Church was named. Her relatives looked forward to receiving Aunt Hattie's fruitcakes every Christmas.

Lemon Cake

³/₄ cup Wesson oil

4 eggs, whole

1 box lemon Jello

³/₄ cup apricot nectar

1 box yellow cake mix

Put all above in mixer and mix well. Bake 1 hour at 325 degrees.

ICING:

      Juice and grated rind of 1 lemon

      1 to 2 cups powdered sugar, or enough to make desired consistency

Mix and pour over the cake while it is still warm.

GEORGIA BELLE GILL

JANE CREASE BOHLINGER BRETT was born in 1900. She was a long-time member of the Mount Holly Board and a delightful character. She hugged everybody she knew; and one day when a friend took her to lunch, she got up and hugged a lady walking by and they had a pleasant conversation. When the lady left, the friend asked who she was and Jane said, "I've no idea." She was also a good cook; and when she had to go to a nursing home, she tried in vain to go to the kitchen and show them how to improve the meals.

An Epitaph for Jane Brett by Archie House

Here lies the kind-hearted and exuberant Jane Brett

Who, habitually hugged and kissed every friend she met.

Alas! One day an Iranian robot sneaked into view.

Poor Jane! She thought it was a friend she knew.

The ensuing explosion was so catastrophic and loud

It necessitated the purchase of a burial shroud.

On earth, Jane was cheerful, chatty, convivial and jolly

But now she rests quietly in her beloved Mount Holly.

Jane Brett's Prune Cake

3 eggs, beaten

1 cup Wesson oil

2 tsp. cinnamon

1 cup buttermilk, beaten with 1 tsp. soda

2 cups cut-up, cooked prunes

2 cups sugar

2 tsp. nutmeg

2 tsp. allspice

2 cups flour with pinch of salt

2 cups chopped pecans

Mix and bake in 300 degree oven for 1 hour or until done.

This is a favorite of relatives and friends.

JUDGE PAT MEHAFFY was Chief Judge for the United States Court of Appeals for the Eighth Circuit, serving as Chief Judge beginning in 1973. He was nominated to the seat by President John F. Kennedy and approved by the U. S. Senate in 1963. Earlier, he had served as Attorney General for the state of Arkansas and as Prosecuting Attorney of Pulaski County; and he was one of the founders of the law firm Mehaffy, Smith & Williams (now The Friday Firm, largest in the state).

Katie Mehaffy's Pound Cake

2 cups sugar	2 sticks butter
1 egg	5 eggs
2 cups sifted flour	2 Tbs. almond flavoring

Cream butter, sugar, and 1 egg in a mixer for a long time until puffy. Sift flour and add to the sugar mixture, alternating between flour and then an egg. Add almond flavoring, mixing well. Put in a greased pan with a bit of additional flour sifted over the pan. Bake in 350 degree preheated oven for 1 hour.

WILLIAM JENNINGS SMITH was aide to five governors and often referred to as "the other governor" or "assistant governor in charge of influence." In 1945, under Governor Laney, his proudest achievement was co-authoring the Arkansas Revenue and Stabilization Act and General Accounting and Procedures Laws which required the state to have a balanced budget. This Act laid the groundwork for the state's fiscal solvency to this day. The construction of the Governor's Mansion, War Memorial Stadium, and the restoration of the Old State House took place during this time.

Under Governor Faubus he created the Act 9 bond program, which helped bring an influx of industry. He also served as an Associate Justice of the Arkansas Supreme Court.

Angel Food Cake

1 cup cake flour, sifted 7 times	1 cup sugar, sifted 7 times
1 cup egg whites (8 to 10 eggs)	1 tsp. cream of tartar
$3/4$ tsp. vanilla	$1/8$ tsp. salt

Beat egg whites and salt with flat wire whip. When foamy add cream of tartar. Beat the eggs until peak will form. Fold in sugar and then fold in the flour. Add flavoring, pour batter into ungreased angel food tube cake pan. Bake in slow oven (275 degrees) for about one hour. Remove from oven and invert pan on its legs or over a bottle until cold. Remove from pan onto rack or plate, ice if desired.

Gold Cake

$1/2$ cup butter	$1 1/2$ cups sugar
9 egg yolks, well beaten	1 cup milk
2 tsp. baking powder	$2 1/2$ cups flour
1 tsp. lemon or vanilla extract	

Cream butter and sugar. Add well-beaten egg yolks and beat thoroughly. Add milk alternately with flour that has been sifted with baking powder. Beat well. Bake 40 minutes in tube pan in 325 degree oven. Ice if desired with orange icing made with butter, powdered sugar and grated rind of one orange and enough orange juice to give spreading consistency.

(These always go together as the angel uses the whites and the gold the yolks of the egg.)

Coming to Little Rock in 1836, when Arkansas became a state, JOHN WASSELL was hired as the contractor to finish the State Capitol building. Because there was no available housing for him and his wife, they settled in the second floor of the west wing of the unfinished capitol until they could find an appropriate house. When the legislature met for its first session, the time limit under Wassell's contract was near and he was far from through. He put carpenters on the roof, immediately above the legislative halls; and they created such a din that Wassell was hailed before the senate and told to call off his carpenters. He replied that he would be unable to fulfill his contract unless the work was allowed to progress. After some negotiation he was given a contract for three years more if he would call off his workmen—which he, of course, did.

During the Civil War, Wassell was living at Commerce and Markham streets when General Steel's army was approaching the city. Wassell went to see the mayor, who lived close by and was sick in bed. It was about 9 a.m.; and James A. Henry, another well-known resident and an alderman, was also there. The mayor asked Henry and Wassell to take the sheet from his bed and wave it before the advancing cavalry, thus surrendering the city of Little Rock on September 18, 1863.

In 1867, the School for the Deaf was started by John Wassell and two others in a rented house on Third Street; and they paid all expenses for several years. Finally the legislature made an appropriation to buy land and erect a permanent school. Wassell was asked to select the site, which is where it is today. There was a lot of opposition to it because "it was so far away, and Little Rock would never grow to it."

Arkansas's Old State House (State Capitol Building in 1836)

Ruth Wassell Woodward's Fudge Cake

Sift and set aside:

> 1 cup sugar and 1 cup flour

Combine and bring to a boil:

> $\frac{1}{4}$ cup butter ($\frac{1}{2}$ stick)   2 Tbs. cocoa
>
> $\frac{1}{2}$ cup water

Add sugar and flour mixture. Add 1 egg, unbeaten. Add $\frac{1}{3}$ cup buttermilk and $\frac{3}{4}$ tsp. soda mixed. Add 1 Tbs. vanilla. Mix well and bake at 350 degrees in an 8" square pan for 25 minutes or until done.

ICING:

> 1 cup sugar   2 Tbs. cocoa
>
> 1 Tbs. butter   6 Tbs. milk

Add a little vanilla extract and bring to a boil for 3 minutes. Beat and pour over cake.

RUTH WASSELL WOODWARD was born in 1879. She was a genealogical historian and served for many years on the Mount Holly board. She was a sister of World War II hero, Dr. Corydon Wassell (buried in Arlington), who was awarded the Navy Cross for "courageous action and devotion to duty in the successful evacuation of wounded under his charge from Java under extremely hazardous and trying conditions" in March 1942. A movie was made of his life, "The Story of Dr. Wassell."

To make delicious bread the citizens of Little Rock could have had their grain ground at the mill of MAJOR ISAAC WATKINS. In 1822 the major announced the completion of the city's first horse mill which could grind "fifty bushels of good meal a day," a vast improvement over the former hand mills.

Buried in an old fashioned box-shaped tomb at Mount Holly, Major Watkins was born in Virginia in 1777, fought in the War of 1812 (hence the "Major"), and came to Arkansas with his wife Maria in 1820. The family lived in a log cabin while Isaac built the city's first frame house, which he ran as a public house called The Little Rock Tavern.

In addition to his town house Isaac developed a large farm north of the river where he built the county's first brick house. When visiting his farm one morning he discovered that some of his stock was missing. Hogs were an important part of the economy; for most of the century, meat meant pork. Tracing the carcass of one of his hogs to the cabin of a neighbor, John Smith, he accused Smith of the theft. At the time Smith did not appear to resent this.

MARIA WATKINS noted in her diary the next morning her husband could not keep his adoring eyes away from her. (A premonition?) Afterward he went to McLane's General Store and it was there that Smith entered, "put his rifle to a charge," and killed Isaac Watkins. In the ensuing confusion Smith leaped on his horse and rode away with a posse belatedly on his trail. Despite the $575 reward offered for his apprehension, Smith escaped twice and was never brought to justice.

Isaac Watkins's wife Maria was the second white woman to live in Little Rock. When she died at the age of 81 her obituary noted that she was "the oldest female resident of our city."

Fresh Apple Cake

3 cups sifted flour

2 cups sugar

1 tsp. cinnamon

1 tsp. soda

1 tsp. salt

Mix together in a large bowl with spoon. Add 1 1/2 cups oil and 2 beaten eggs and mix. Add 3 cups chopped apple (peeled) and 1 1/2 cups chopped pecans. Mix with hands. Put in greased and floured bundt pan and cook at 350 degrees for one hour. Cool on rack, then remove to plate.

GOVERNOR FRANK WHITE surprised his wife, Gay, one Christmas. Gay had urged him to make plans for "the future." She said he really did not like to think about it. One day before Christmas he came home and told her he had a surprise for her and made her put on a blindfold. Then he put her in the car and drove to Mount Holly. When he took off her blindfold she saw her gift, a plot of ground at Mount Holly.

Carrot Cake

Mix in large bowl:

> 2 cups sugar   1 $^1/_2$ cups oil

Add:

> 5 eggs – one at a time

Sift together the ingredients below and add in small amounts to above.

> 2 cups flour   2 tsp. baking powder
>
> 1 tsp. soda   2 tsp. cinnamon
>
> $^1/_2$ tsp. salt

Blend in:

> 2 tsp. vanilla   2 cups grated carrots
>
> 1 cup crushed pineapple, well drained.

Bake in 3 greased and floured 9" pans 30 to 40 minutes at 350 degrees.

ICING:

> 8 oz. cream cheese, softened

Add:

> $^1/_2$ cup melted butter   1 lb. powdered sugar
>
> 2 tsp. vanilla

Beat all together.

Sponge Cake
(Excellent)

Six eggs

Half the weight of the eggs in flour

Weight of the eggs in sugar

Juice and rind of 1 lemon

After weighing the sugar and flour, separate the eggs. Beat the yolks and sugar together until very light. Now add the juice and rind of the lemon, and half the flour. Beat the whites to a stiff froth, add half of them to the cake, then the remaining half of the flour, and then the remaining half of the whites; stir lightly, and pour into a greased pan. Bake in a quick oven **45** minutes.

This is a Woodruff family recipe as recorded. Weighing six eggs, we think 1 lb. or 2 cups of sugar and 1 cup of flour would work.

Cookies

Christmas Sugar Cookies

1 lb. butter

5 cups all-purpose flour

Pinch of salt

1 tsp. baking soda dissolved in 3 Tbs. milk

2 eggs

2 cups sugar

1 Tbs. vanilla

Put all ingredients in a bowl and mix with hands until a smooth dough is formed. Form into a ball, dust with flour and chill thoroughly. After chilled, break dough into conveniently sized pieces, adding a little more flour to each bit of dough to make it easier to handle and roll out.

Roll out as thin as possible, dust with granulated sugar and nutmeg and cut into shapes. Bake until light brown in 350 degree oven (about 12 minutes). Ground almonds or nuts of any sort may be added to all or part of the dough. These cookies can be made far in advance and kept in tin boxes in a cool place. Makes 5 to 6 dozen.

DAVID O. DODD, a folk hero of Arkansas history, was executed as a Confederate spy by the Union army in 1864. David had been living in Little Rock with his family until 1862 when he went with his father to Monroe, Louisiana. There he was employed in a telegraph office that had been taken over by the Confederate army, but in December of 1863 David was sent home to Arkansas. The purpose of the trip was to solicit funds from friends in Little Rock who might want to invest in a business venture the father planned. His father sent with him a Confederate pass and a note citing his date and place of birth as evidence that he was too young to be in the army.

After delivering the letters for his father, he remained at the home of his aunt with plans to leave Little Rock on December 28; but he attended a dance and left on the morning of December 29th instead. Mounted on a mule, he headed south with the intention of trading his mule for a horse at the home of a Mr. Davis. Before reaching the home of Davis, David was stopped by Union pickets and arrested. When pressed for identification David produced a book of memoranda that had dots and dashes on the pages, later translated as a catalog of the Federal forces in Little Rock.

David's trial began the next day in Little Rock, where he was charged with gathering military information and "did otherwise lurk, and act as a spy." At his trial the telegraphic symbols were translated; and the final witness for the prosecution stated that the Federal military forces were, with slight variations, as David had recorded them. His defense noted that David could have avoided the pickets if he had wanted to and included a plea for mercy for a boy so young that he had never been connected with the Confederate army. The verdict was guilty. David was hanged on January 8 on the parade ground in front of St. John's College, where he had once been a student.

The funeral was held the next morning, and David was buried at Mount Holly that afternoon in a friend's lot. Through donations a marble shaft and slab were purchased soon after the war ended. Below the inscription giving his name and dates of birth and death is the same inscription chiseled in telegraphic code. The young boy's death was ghoulish enough, but through the years it was embellished through stories of the villains who caused it in various ways and poems describing his heroic deportment on the gallows.

Shortly before time for his funeral to begin, an order came from Union headquarters that the body should be buried without ceremony. Not a word was to be said over his casket, only three mourners allowed to attend, and no music to be played. Today it is one of the most visited graves in the cemetery, and each year in January the Sons of the Confederacy hold a memorial service at the site.

ELOISE LENOW MURPHY was the daughter of Dr. James and Ella Davis Lenow. Gifted in good taste, she became an interior decorator and bought and restored the Old Stagecoach House in 1946, using the house as a basis for her interior decorating operations. The Old Stagecoach House, known as the Ten Mile House, is where Confederate martyr David O. Dodd was kept before he was tried and hanged. (Photo below.)

Potato Chip Cookies

2 sticks butter, room temp.

$^1/_2$ cup sugar

1 $^1/_2$ cups flour

1 tsp. vanilla

1 cup pecans (optional, but better with)

$^3/_4$ cup potato chips, rolled out fine

Drop on cookie sheet, bake at 350 degrees for 15 – 20 minutes.

(These are good, quick and easy. If dropped by teaspoon they will only take 10–11 minutes in convection oven.)

Caramel Squares

1 cup sugar

1 egg

1 tsp. baking powder

1 tsp. vanilla

$^1/_2$ cup butter

1 $^1/_2$ cup flour

Pinch salt

Mix all ingredients and spread in greased pan.

Cover with following mixture:

1 egg white, stiffly beaten

$^1/_2$ cup walnuts or pecans, broken up

1 cup brown sugar

Bake in slow oven, 300 degrees for 40 minutes.

MARION VINSONHALER McCAIN

Mildred Bass's Lapp Cookies

$^1/_2$ lb. butter (2 sticks)

1 $^1/_2$ cups sugar

3 eggs or 5 yolks

$^3/_4$ cup dark Karo

$^1/_2$ lb. chopped pecans

2 oz. chocolate squares or 6 Tbs. cocoa

3 cups flour

2 tsp. baking powder

2 $^1/_2$ tsp. cinnamon

$^1/_2$ tsp. cloves

$^1/_2$ tsp. allspice

Cream butter, add sugar, eggs, Karo, flour sifted with other dry ingredients, and melted chocolate. Drop from teaspoon on greased baking sheet. Bake at 350 degrees.

FREDERIC TRAPNALL, born in Kentucky in 1807, married Martha Cocke on the bride's sixteenth birthday in 1836. After coming to Arkansas Frederic was an attorney, merchant, member of the legislature, and active in the formation of Christ Episcopal Church, the first Episcopal church in Arkansas. Frederic and Martha built Trapnall Hall, one of the few brick houses in Little Rock at that time, and it was there that members of the Whig Party gathered for political meetings. While campaigning for Congress in 1853 Frederic died, but his widow remained in the house until her death in 1863.

MARTHA TRAPNALL apparently had political convictions of her own. On May 6, 1861, the delegates to the Arkansas Secession Convention voted to leave the Union and join the Confederate States of America. It was hoped that the vote would be unanimous; but at the final roll call Isaac Murphy remained firm, saying that after considering the consequences he could not change his vote, and therefore voted "no". The room filled with angry shouts of "Traitor", but in the midst of this a bouquet of flowers was thrown towards Murphy and landed at his feet. The flowers were thrown from the balcony by Martha Trapnall in appreciation of Murphy's stand.

Both Frederic and Martha are buried at Mount Holly; and today their historic home—Trapnall Hall—serves as the Official Receiving Hall for the governors of the State of Arkansas. (Photo below.)

Pecan Tassies

1 package (8 oz.) cream cheese   2 sticks of butter

2 cups sifted flour

Cream butter and cheese. Add flour (1/2 cup at a time), mix and chill, then mash into shape in small muffin tins.

Bake 425 degrees – 15 minutes or 350 degrees – 30 minutes.

FILLING:

3 eggs, well beaten   1 cup of white Karo

$^1/_8$ tsp. salt   1 tsp. vanilla

1 cup sugar   Chopped pecans

Put 1 tsp. or more of chopped pecans in each shell. Fill with Karo nut filling, not too full. Cook at 400 degrees for 15-20 minutes or until done.

A professional landscaper, LOUIE SANFORD was the founder of the Arkansas Federation of Garden Clubs, Inc. and editor of *The Arkansas Gardener* for 30 years. Upon graduation with a degree in horticulture from Smith College, Louie saw to it that a pecan orchard was planted on her parents' cotton farm, Illallee Plantation in Scott. This recipe was her favorite.

Molasses Cookies

Woodruff Family

1 cup molasses

1/2 cup sugar

1 level Tbs. ginger

1/4 cup cold water

1/4 cup butter

1/2 level tsp. salt

1/2 level tsp. soda

4 cups flour

Scald molasses, pour it over butter, sugar, salt, and ginger. Dissolve soda in water, add to the cooled molasses, then stir in flour, making a stiff dough to be rolled and cut. Bake in moderate oven (375 degrees.)

Lemon Squares

CRUST:

2 cups flour

1 cup soft butter

1/2 cup powdered sugar

FILLING:

4 eggs

1/3 cup fresh lemon juice

1/2 tsp. baking powder

2 cups sugar

1/4 cup flour

Sift flour and powdered sugar. Cut butter into dry mixture until crumbly. Press into a greased 9 x 13 pan. Bake at 350 degrees for 25-30 minutes or until light brown. (Do not overcook.)

Combine eggs, sugar, and lemon juice. Sift flour and baking powder and add to filling. Pour over baked crust and bake an additional 25 – 30 minutes at 350.

Gingerbread

1 cup sorghum molasses	1 cup sugar
1 1/4 cups butter	1 cup buttermilk
2 eggs	2 1/2 cups sifted flour
1 Tbs. powdered ginger	1 Tbs. cinnamon
1 Tbs. powdered cloves	1 1/4 tsp. nutmeg
2 tsp. soda	

Mix all together, saving the soda until last. Bake in two layer pans, or in a 7 x 12 layer pan, at 350 degrees for about 40 minutes.

SAUCE:

1/2 lb. brown sugar	2 Tbs. flour
Water to wet good	

Boil about 5 minutes.

ALTERNATE SAUCE: LEMON SAUCE

1 cup sugar	1/4 cup water
3 Tbs. lemon juice	1 lemon rind, grated
1 egg	1/2 cup butter

Melt 1/2 cup butter in saucepan. Remove from heat to add sugar, water, lemon juice, and rind. Beat egg and stir into sugar-water mixture. Cook over medium heat, stirring constantly until boiling. Serve warm. May be refrigerated and reheated to serve over cake or pudding.

The stonemason JAMES McVICAR was a true adventurer. Having come to the United States from Scotland, he came to Arkansas with two other Scotsmen in 1837 to work as stonemasons on the new State House. In 1842 he built his own home that is still standing in the territorial capitol area, preserved as part of the Historic Arkansas Museum. When the Mexican War began, he joined the troops. After the war he returned to Little Rock, just as the gold rush began. Anxious for another adventure, he organized a company to go overland to California.

They set out from Van Buren, Arkansas, "leaving for the land of the gold." The local newspapers, anticipating the amount of cooking necessary on the trail, advertised "Tin Ware for California," promising "pots and kettles that will be useful, as they can be used on the road and will do to wash gold in after arriving in California." They also took flour and bacon for the prospectors and corn for the horses.

McVicar's luck in California was in trading, not mining—using his profits for large land purchases. He returned to Arkansas to marry Amanda Miller, took his new wife to California, and returned to Little Rock in 1869. Three years later he was buried in a Masonic lot at Mount Holly.

Shortbread

1 cup butter

½ cup granulated sugar

2 cups all purpose flour

Place butter in large bowl and knead with hands, squeezing between fingers until smooth and creamy, not oily. (May use spoon to smear butter around until no lumps remain.) Gradually cream sugar in butter with hands or spoon. Work in flour, kneading it with fingers or stirring with spoon. Work only until flour has been absorbed. Shape dough into 8" circle on ungreased baking sheet and decorate the edge with tines of kitchen fork. Place in a 350 degree oven. Cook 15 minutes to 20 minutes until edges of shortbread are just beginning to brown.

Should a thinner, crisper shortbread be desired, shape dough into a dish and refrigerate 1 hour or overnight. Roll out on a lightly floured board to a little less than ¼ inch. Transfer to baking sheet and cook 10-15 minutes at 350 degrees. Serve in pieces broken off of whole.

McVicar-Conway House, 1948
From the permanent collection of the Historic Arkansas Museum

Pogahtcha Cookies

Grind 2 cups almonds or pecans, cream 2 sticks of butter, 1 cup of sugar, then add 2 whole eggs and $1\frac{1}{4}$ cups of almonds. Add 2 cups of flour and mix well. Roll batter thin, about like biscuits, and place cookies, round or square, in a greased pan. Brush with 1 egg yolk and sprinkle with $\frac{1}{4}$ cup nuts, $\frac{1}{4}$ cup sugar, and $\frac{1}{4}$ cup grated orange peel. Bake in medium oven. (Use medium grater for orange peel.)

The Public Mauseleum was designed by architect Charles Thompson and built in 1919. It has 165 crypts and is listed in the National Register of Historic Places.

Pies, Puddings & Such

The idea of the XV Club (a gentlemen's club) was brought to Little Rock in 1903 from Pine Bluff where it was organized with the same name and plan by Reverend J. L. Caldwell, pastor of First Presbyterian Church of Pine Bluff. The first meeting in Little Rock was held at the home of H. L. Remmel on January 7, 1904 with 15 members. The club met bi-monthly having a gourmet dinner followed by good cigars and the presentation of papers on a designated subject by two members, each allotted a half hour. The meetings adjourned after a bit over 3 hours with the guests learning the topics of the next meeting.

Members dress formally, no alcohol is served, and everything is done by numbers. There are 15 semi-monthly meetings with the first, also attended by wives, being in the fall and the last in May. If the host of the first meeting of the year is No. 1, the host of the first meeting the next year will be No. 2 and so on. Similarly, the only two officers, the Squire (President) and Scribe (Secretary) rotate among the members in numerical order. It is bad form not to respond to meeting invitations in time to allow for the invitation of guests to fill the vacancies so there will be 15 in attendance. Members are referred to only by their numbers.

The dinners are very formal with certain members serving traditional dinners. Judge McFaddin always served the following menu: tomato consommé, oysters Rockefeller, quail, salad and a dessert of ice cream, whipped cream and Matilda's raspberry sauce (Mrs. McFaddin's specialty).

Raspberry Sauce

2 (10 oz.) packages frozen raspberries   1 Tbs. cornstarch
2 Tbs. water   ½ cup kirsch (liqueur)

Bring raspberries to a boil. Add mixture of cornstarch and water and cook until sauce is clear. Strain sauce, then add kirsch. Cool. This may also be served hot. To make an uncooked sauce, puree raspberries in electric blender or food mill. Add kirsch; omit cornstarch.

Lemon Ice Cream

11 cups light cream

4 cups sugar

1 Tbs. grated lemon rind.

Juice of 8 lemons

2 tsp. lemon extract

Mix and freeze in your freezer, stirring once when partially frozen or freeze in your ice cream freezer. Great summer dessert.

DR. ROBERT WATSON was considered the "father of neurosurgery in Arkansas." He began his neurosurgery practice in 1942, and anyone needing neurosurgery no longer had to look beyond the state. In 1944 he became the 108th physician to receive accreditation from the American Board of Neurological Society. For 27 years, he volunteered as a teacher to educate young physicians about diagnosing neurological cases. His wife, known as P. L. D. WATSON, served on the Mount Holly Board for many years.

Dr. Watson's Custard Ice Cream

2 cups scalded milk (whole milk)

4 egg yolks, beaten

1 Tbs. vanilla

1 cup sugar

$\frac{1}{8}$ tsp. salt

1 qt. half and half cream

Mix sugar, salt, and beaten egg yolks. Add milk to mixture gradually. Cook in double boiler for 10 minutes, stirring constantly. When totally cool (ice box cool), add cream and vanilla.

Freeze in ice cream freezer.

P. L. D. Watson's Charlotte Russe

¹/₂ cup water	2 envelopes Knox (plain) gelatin
4 egg yolks	1 cup sugar
Pinch salt	1 ³/₄ cups scalded milk
1 tsp. sherry extract	1 tsp. vanilla
¹/₄ cup sherry	4 egg whites
1 pint whipping cream	1 box Lady Fingers

Line a deep bowl with Lady Fingers (split). Soften gelatin in water. (Set aside.) Scald milk. Beat egg yolks with sugar and salt. Stir in milk. Place all in double boiler over simmering water. Cook until thicker and it coats a spoon. Stir constantly. Do not over cook or it will curdle. Pour immediately over gelatin and stir until dissolved. Cool in refrigerator. When it begins to set, fold in flavorings and sherry. Beat egg whites with a pinch of salt until peaks form. (Beaters must be totally clean.) Whip cream. Fold all three together. Refrigerate until slightly thicker. Pour into Lady Finger-lined bowl. Refrigerate until set. Decorate with sliced cherries to resemble a poinsettia. (The sherry and the sherry extract can be omitted, if you wish.)

This Charlotte Russe was a Christmas tradition from P.L.D.'s childhood that has been handed down to her children. Kids love it. Adults love it. Serve at Christmas Dinner.

Boiled Christmas Custard

Sowell Family Recipe

1 quart milk	4 large eggs	¼ cup sugar
2 Tbs. all purpose-flour	2 tsps. vanilla extract	

Heat the milk in a heavy non-aluminum saucepan over medium heat (or in a double boiler) until the milk is hot. Combine the eggs, sugar, and flour in a small bowl and beat until blended well. Gradually stir a cup of the hot milk into the egg mixture and then add all of the egg mixture back into the hot milk. Stir constantly.

Continue to cook over medium heat, stirring constantly until the mixture begins to thicken. Remove from the heat. If lumps have formed, pour through a strainer to remove them. Top with plastic wrap to prevent a "skin" from forming on the top. Chill.

This recipe handed down in Martha Sowell's family was prepared each year and served at Christmas time. It was also prepared as a remedy for sick friends as it was felt that it gave them nourishment to help them have a speedy recovery.

Virginia Alexander's Baked Custard

4 egg yolks, beaten but "not too much"		1 pint of cream, scalded
4 Tbs. of sugar	1 tsp. vanilla	Dash of salt

Put in Pyrex custard cups in pan with a small amount of water surrounding cups. Bake at 350 degrees for 40 minutes or until knife comes out clean.

Virginia is known for taking these custards to shut-ins at All Souls Church as a comfort food. This church was built the year Virginia was born (1907). She baked these custards every Sunday afternoon to share with friends up until her 100th birthday.

JAMES ANTHONY DIBRELL, JR. M.D. was born in 1846 in Van Buren. His father was a doctor, as were two brothers and two sons. He was ready to enter college when the Civil War started, and all schools in this part of the country were closed. During the war his father lost everything and was not able to continue his son's education. However, Dibrell was determined to be a doctor and began working in the state auditor's department to earn money. He worked during the day and studied with his father at night; and by the winter of 1867-68 he was able to take a course at St. Louis Medical College. The following year he entered the Department of Medicine at the University of Pennsylvania from which he received his degree in 1870. After graduation he took another series of lectures there. He married LALLIE REARDON in 1876.

Dr. Dibrell returned to Little Rock and began a successful practice. He was active in all the medical organizations and was one of the founders of the Medical Department of the University of Arkansas and was dean of the school for twenty years. He was also vice-president of the American Medical Association. As secretary of the state board of health he worked hard during the yellow fever epidemic of 1879-80, and Arkansas escaped the terrible disease. He invented several surgical instruments and was widely known and respected. He died in 1904.

Little Rock's first hospital was organized in the early 1870's with two Mount Holly residents, Dr. James A. Dibrell and Dr. James H. Lenow, as the physicians-in-charge. The Panic of 1873 hit the south and west hard and left many citizens unable to pay their bills to the few doctors in town. Blackberries were free, and those who couldn't pay their medical bills often sent buckets filled to the brim with freshly picked blackberries to Dr. Dibrell for payment.

1850 Blackberry Pie

1 unbaked 10" pie shell   1 qt. blackberries

1 cup flour   2 cups sugar

1 cup milk

Fill shell with berries. Mix flour, sugar, and milk. Pour mixture over berries. Bake at 350 degrees for 45 – 50 minutes, until center is set. If desired, brown under broiler.

8 servings

Blackberry Cobbler

FILLING:

    1 cup sugar

    1 cup hot water

    2 heaping Tbs. cornstarch

    4 cups blackberries

Mix sugar and cornstarch in saucepan and slowly add hot water, stirring to dissolve. Bring to boil and cook until thick and clear. Cool slightly, add berries and stir. Pour into 10 x 14 baking dish.

TOPPING:

    1 cup all purpose flour

    $^1/_4$ cup sugar

    1 stick butter

    1 tsp. vanilla extract

    2 tsp. baking powder

    pinch salt

    $^1/_2$ cup milk

Sift flour, baking powder, sugar, and salt together in mixing bowl. Crumble in butter. Beat until mixture forms small granules. Add milk to make thick like cake batter. Add vanilla and stir. Pour over berry mixture. Bake at 350 degrees 25 -30 minutes. Test with toothpick.

Fruit Cobbler

1 qt. sweetened fruit (such as large can of peaches)

¼ lb. butter	1 cup flour	1 cup sugar
1 tsp. baking powder	¼ tsp. salt	1 cup milk

Heat fruit in saucepan. Have butter melted in 2 qt. casserole. Mix flour, sugar, baking powder, and salt and stir in milk. Beat until smooth. Pour cake-like mixture into casserole. Do not stir. Pour hot fruit in middle and do not stir. Bake at 350 degrees for 1 hour.

This cobbler was a favorite of GENE CRAWFORD, the husband of Sybil Crawford, who is the historian of Mount Holly and author of Jubilee. The recipe was given to Sybil in the 50s by a neighbor who had received it from her mother-in-law.

LEON LEFEVRE, thought to be Arkansas's oldest native-born resident, was born at Arkansas Post in 1808 and resided in the state until his death. He was a farmer who had no desire for city life. He was the son of Peter LeFevre, who migrated from Canada to his Spanish land grant at the former French Post of Arkansas in 1789.

Maple Mousse

1 cup maple syrup	4 eggs
Few grains of salt	2 cups whipping cream
1 tsp. vanilla	

Pour syrup over beaten eggs, add salt and cook in top of double boiler until thick. Cool. Add cream, whipped, and vanilla. Turn into mold or ramekins and put in freezer for 8 hours. When serving, garnish with whipped cream and crushed peanut brittle.

In 1819 PETER LEFEVRE moved with his 5 sons "near Little Rock" (Baucum) when he purchased the Bartholomew grant on the north side of the river. He built a home and landing, died in 1820, and was buried in the nearby family cemetery. The 1927 flood threatened the plots; and in a charitable effort, Charles Lockerts, a kinsman, removed the bones and tombstone to his front lawn to dry. Cousin Eudie LeFevre (Mrs. Anderson Mills) was outraged that her grandfather's bones were exposed on his former plantation's lawn where, it was said, that they were hung on a tree. With much ado they were reinterred in his son Leon LeFevre's Mount Holly lot in 1927.

Maple Syrup Pie

CRUST:

1 cup flour	¼ tsp. salt	1 tsp. sugar
5 Tbs. Butter, cubed	3 Tbs. Ice water	

FILLING:

2 eggs	1 Tbs. Flour	½ cup heavy cream
1 cup maple syrup, preferably medium dark		Creme fraiche, for serving.

Preheat the oven to 400 degrees. Make crust by combining flour, salt, and sugar in a large bowl. Cut the butter into the flour with a fork or pastry blender until the mixture is the texture of coarse meal. Sprinkle a Tbs. of ice water at a time over the dough, lifting and tossing it with the fork. When it begins to come together, gather the dough, press it into a ball and then pull it apart. If it crumbles in your hands, it needs more water. Add a tsp. or two more water, as needed.

Flatten the ball of dough and roll between two sheets of plastic wrap into a circle 10 " in diameter. Remove the plastic and lay dough into a 9" tart pan, press into place and remove excess dough. Place in the freezer.

Meanwhile, make the filling by beating the eggs in a bowl. Gradually whisk in the flour. Add the cream and maple syrup and whisk until combined. Pour into the crust-lined pan. Cook until the middle still jiggles but is solid, 25 to 30 minutes. Serve with crème fraiche. Serves 12.

MARY HAMILTON PIKE (MRS. ALBERT PIKE) was born in 1816 at Arkansas Post. She married Albert Pike, a brilliant drop-out from Harvard, in 1834. Three months later she inherited a substantial estate of $2,500, which Albert immediately relieved her of to buy the *Arkansas Advocate* from Charles Bertrand. With this purchase Pike became the senior editor, along with being an attorney. This was arranged by Crittenden to further his campaign against the dynasty of Democrats. Pike's first edition of the *Arkansas Advocate* was on January 20, 1835.

Albert Pike built a fine mansion, but was in it less and less with his involvement in the Mexican War, work with the Indians, and the Civil War. Somewhere along the way he translated the Napoleonic code into English and moved permanently to Washington after the Civil War to work full time with the Masons.

Mrs. Pike moved out of the big house into a smaller one. Three of their children died before they were grown; and Mrs. Pike died on April 14, 1876, at the age of 60. Albert is buried in Washington D. C.

Pike was a distant cousin of Zebulon Pike, for whom Pike County is named.

Not all duels ended tragically. In 1847 Albert Pike challenged John Roane to a duel and the two met on a sand bar of the Arkansas River (in an area that was at that time Indian Territory). There was a large crowd, including a number of Indians, and Pike smoked a cigar to show how calm he was as the seconds loaded the pistols. On the second round of shots each grazed the other; and although the seconds could not call a halt (since this would impugn the honor of their own party), the two surgeons could and did, announcing: "They shan't fire again. Unless they make this quarrel up, we will just go away and leave them to hurt each other as much as they want, and not be on hand to help them." This caused the two duelers to shake hands, bury the past, and become good friends.

A Plain Pudding

Peel 6 tart apples and grate into dish. Add equal quantity grated bread crumbs. Beat 2 eggs, add 2 cups milk, 3 Tbs. sugar, and a dash of salt. Flavor with grated lemon or orange peel. Pour on first mixture, stir well and bake until set at 350 degrees.

CHARLES KNOX LINCOLN was born in 1871 and married Irma Culbert in 1917. They had four children. He was a Mason, a member of the Boathouse, the McCarthy Light Guards, and president of the wholesale drug firm, McKesson Lincoln Co., later McKesson and Robbins Co.

IRMA CULBERT LINCOLN was born in 1893. She was a charter member of the Junior League of Little Rock, and president 1926-1928. Their elegant Victorian house at Seventh and Cumberland, built by his parents, is still standing and is lovingly cared for by its present owners.

Old Fashioned Cobbler

3 cups peeled, sliced peaches

2 tsp. lemon juice

2 Tbs. butter

2 Tbs. white sugar

$^1/_4$ tsp. salt

$^1/_3$ cup salad oil

$^1/_2$ cup brown sugar

$^1/_2$ tsp. almond extract

1 $^1/_2$ cups flour

$^1/_2$ tsp. baking powder

$^1/_3$ cup benne seed or sesame seed

3 Tbs. milk

Place peaches in a buttered baking dish, sprinkle with brown sugar, lemon juice, almond extract, and dot with butter. Sift together flour, white sugar, baking powder, and salt. Beat oil and milk together and stir into flour mixture with seeds. Roll out between two sheets of wax paper, fit over peaches, and cut slits in top. Bake at 375 degrees about 40 minutes or until top is brown. Sprinkle with 1 Tbs. sugar, 2 tsp. butter, and continue cooking for 5 minutes.

LOUISE HEISKELL PATTERSON served on the Board of the *Arkansas Gazette* and was a leader of civic and cultural affairs in the state. Her father, John Heiskell, was president and editor of the *Arkansas Gazette* from 1902 until his death in 1972. Although Louise was not involved in operation of the newspaper on a daily basis, she was a participant in decision making behind the scenes. She considered herself a representative of the family legacy; and through their philosophy and independent thinking, she helped form the newspaper's conscience. Louise was stalwart through the *Gazette's* most difficult years—the desegregation crisis—and in 1987, Hugh and Louise Patterson were co-recipients of the Humanitarian Award of the Arkansas Council on Brotherhood of the National Conference of Christians and Jews. Former Vice President Walter F. Mondale lauded them as "heroes" for helping to successfully engineer "the most peaceful social revolution in American society." He said that with their involvement in the newspaper's role in support of law and order during the 1957 desegregation crisis at Central High School, "they risked their personal fortune and perhaps their lives."

Louise was an authority on Christmas nativity scenes and published a reference pamphlet on the history of the crèche. She was a noted hostess and often prepared all the food for annual Christmas open house parties and other social occasions at her home.

Louise Heiskell Patterson served a cake flavored with Triple Sec that was delicious. The recipe called for ¼ cup of the liqueur. She tasted it, and it didn't have enough; so she kept adding and finally emptied the whole bottle. No wonder it was so good!

Cold Grand Marnier Soufflé

½ cup sugar	2 Tbs. gelatin	1 cup milk
6 egg yolks	1 Tbs. grated orange rind	1 cup orange juice
6 egg whites	½ tsp. cream of tartar	½ cup sugar
¼ cup Grand Marnier	1 cup whipping cream	

Combine ½ cup sugar with gelatin, milk, and yolks and cook gently until boiling point, but do not let boil. Cool. Add rind and juice. Chill until mounds form from spoon. Beat whites and cream of tartar until frothy. Beat in ½ cup sugar gradually. When stiff and glossy fold in Grand Marnier and whipped cream. Chill in 1 qt. soufflé dish. Put collar around dish and remove carefully.

EMILY BOURNE, born in 1877, was a founder of the Little Rock Garden Club and a long-time board member of Mount Holly, serving as treasurer for many years. The board met in her home, which was filled with pink satin-covered furniture, until her death in 1961. She was a life member of Women of the Church of the Presbyterian Church of the United States and an aunt of John F. Boyle, Jr., who built the Boyle Building and gave Boyle Park to the city.

Emily's Apple Pie

Unbaked pie crust	4 eggs
Jar of apple jelly	1/4 cup butter, melted
Juice and grated rind of one lemon	1/2 cup cream

Mix ingredients well, pour into the unbaked pie crust and bake for 45 minutes at 325 degrees.

Mrs. W. B. Worthen and her daughters had lunch one day with "Miss Emily" Bourne who lived across the street. Miss Emily liked the color pink and often dyed the rice pink. This day she served asparagus wrapped in a piece of bread and tied with a pink ribbon. Mrs. Worthen was advanced in years and did not see too well at the time and started eating the asparagus, ribbon and all. Her daughters looked on, fascinated, as she devoured the whole thing.

Daisy Keatts's Dessert

Make a custard of 1 qt. milk, ½ cup sugar, 4 egg yolks, and 1 tsp. cornstarch, cooking in top of a double boiler until thick. (Be sure to mix some of the scalded milk with eggs before adding eggs to rest of the scalded milk in double boiler.)

Line a dish with 1 dozen Lady Fingers (soak in some kind of fruit juice or brandy). On top of these put contents of small can crushed pineapple and pour the custard over all. Refrigerate.

"How to Trap a Man" Chocolate Pie

This is a story about young love and the Quapaw Quarter, the neighborhood surrounding Mount Holly. In the summer of 1975, my little sister, Marianne, lived with me while attending summer school at UALR. The Quapaw Quarter is a close-knit community where neighbors often gather for pot-lucks and picnics. At the Memorial Day picnic in the vacant lot next to Paris Towers, Marianne met a young lawyer, Stark Ligon, who had just bought a house in the Quarter. Marianne assured him that she was an excellent cook and promised a gourmet picnic to prove it. That was the start of a summer of elegant picnics and dinner parties surreptitiously cooked by me.

I lived then, as I do now, in a big old house on Gaines Street, though my kitchen then left much to be desired. It was your basic 19th century kitchen. There was a cast iron sink, but no air-conditioning. Throughout the rest of that long, hot summer I cooked while Marianne and Stark nibbled on treats such as this pie while they fell in love under the old oaks of Mount Holly and MacArthur Park. I like to think that my chocolate pie recipe has had something to do with this long and loving marriage.

Matilda Wynne Buchanan

"How To Trap A Man" Chocolate Pie

Pie Filling:

½ cup sugar

1 stick butter

2 eggs beaten

1 Tbs. flour

1 cup dark brown sugar

1 ½ squares unsweetened chocolate

2 Tbs. milk

1 tsp. vanilla

In the top of double boiler, melt the sugars, butter, and chocolate, stirring occasionally. Cool slightly. Mix in other ingredients.

Pie Crust:

If making pie crust, mix together 1 ¼ cups flour and 1 Tbs. sugar. Using a pastry blender, cut in 6 Tbs. butter and 2 Tbs. shortening until mixture resembles coarse meal. Stir in ¼ cup ice water, mix and form a ball of dough. Wrap in plastic wrap and refrigerate for 30 minutes. Then roll out dough on floured surface. Cut and fit into pie plate and refrigerate 20 minutes. If using store bought, set it out following package instructions so that you can roll into pie plate. After placing in pie plate refrigerate 20 minutes.

Preheat oven to 400 degrees.

Line pie crust with foil, fill with dried beans or pie weights, and bake at 400 degrees for 8 to 10 minutes until crust is partially cooked. Remove from oven and reduce heat to 350 degrees. Put filling in partially baked pie shell and bake at 350 degrees for 45 – 50 minutes. Center will be just set. Cool pie on counter and then refrigerate. Pie will be the consistency of fudge and can be served cold or room temperature.

MARY WEBSTER LOUGHBOROUGH became the epitome of "True Grits." Born in New York in 1836, Mary moved as a young girl with her family to St. Louis where she met and married JAMES LOUGHBOROUGH. When the Civil War began, James joined the Confederate army, and Mary followed him as closely as possible, trying to keep the family together. In the summer of 1863 she was living with their two-year-old daughter in Vicksburg, Mississippi, where James was among the troops defending the city. Anxious to control the river, the Union army began bombarding the streets of the city, causing civilians to move for safety into caves dug in the side of nearby cliffs. Mary realized the necessity for this move when, on the first night of the siege, "the room that I had so lately slept in was struck by a fragment of a shell and a large hole was made in the ceiling."

While the Confederate soldiers fought in the trenches, the women and children became captives in the caves. In 1864 Mary wrote a book, My Cave Life in Vicksburg, describing the ordeal: "Our new habitation was an excavation made in the earth, and branching six feet from the entrance, forming a cave in the shape of a T." In one of the wings there was a narrow camp bed; in the other "the earth had been cut down a foot or two below the floor of the main cave. I could stand erect here; and when tired of sitting in other portions of my residence, I bowed myself into it, and stood at full height—one of the variations in the shell-expectant life."

She described their meager food and her dread of the constant bombardment where the shots came in quick succession, "leaving me in the quiet state of terror, the most painful that I can imagine—cowering in a corner, holding my child to my heart." The summer heat increased, "and so the weary days went on—the long and weary days—when we could not tell in what terrible form death might come to us."

On July 3rd a truce was called to discuss surrender, and Mary said that at last she "put on my bonnet and sallied forth beyond the terrace, for the first time since I entered." The earth was covered with fragments of shell of all shapes and kinds, but the siege of Vicksburg was over. Confederate soldiers, after 47 days, laid down their arms on July 4th.

But Mary's days as a true grits woman were not over. After the war James Loughborough, an attorney, brought his family to Little Rock, where he was employed by the railroad. In 1876, at age 43, he had just been elected to the state senate when he died "from the accidental discharge of his gun." His widow, left with three children, needed to support the family. Again she turned to her writing ability as she began publishing the Southern Ladies Journal, dedicated to "the interests and advancement of women."

Mary died in 1887—unfortunately not living to know her son's wife, Louisa Loughborough, who was a prime mover in the restoration of the early territorial buildings that are today the Historic Arkansas Museum.

Chess Pie

2 cups sugar   1 Tbs. flour   1 Tbs. cornmeal

Toss the above together.

Add:

4 eggs   1/4 cup melted butter   1/4 cup milk

4 Tbs. grated lemon rind   1/4 cup lemon juice

Beat until smooth. Pour into unbaked pie shell. Bake for 10 minutes at 400 degrees, then turn down to 350 for 25 minutes.

JAMES LOUGHBOROUGH, SR. worked for the railroad. When they were extending the tracks in south Arkansas, Old Washington would not allow the trains to go through their "clean" city. So they started a new one a few miles away. Mr. Loughborough had just had a new baby whose name was HOPE, so they named the new city for her. She and the city were born in 1869. Hope was also the birthplace of President Bill Clinton.

Chocolate Chess Pie

1/4 cup butter   1 1/2 oz. unsweetened chocolate

1 1/2 cup sugar   1 Tbs. flour   pinch salt

1/2 cup milk   2 eggs   1 tsp. vanilla extract

1 unbaked 9" pastry shell

Melt butter and chocolate and pour into mixing bowl. Add sugar, etc. and beat with electric mixer 6 minutes. Pour in pie shell. Bake at 350 degrees for 40 minutes.

JAMES LOUGHBOROUGH, JR. and his wife, Louisa, lived in south Little Rock near Glenwood Park at 17th and Main Streets. In the summer everyone kept the windows open, and sound as well as fresh air came in. There was a band at the park that frequently played "Waltzing Matilda." Mr. Loughborough said to his wife, "If they play that piece one more time, I am going to move." Of course they did, and he did.

LOUISA WATKINS WRIGHT LOUGHBOROUGH, born in 1881, was a direct descendant of the last Territorial Governor of Arkansas, William Savin Fulton. She served as Vice Regent on the Board of Regents of the Mount Vernon Ladies Association of the Union and was inspired by Anne Pamela Cunningham, who saved George Washington's home 90 years earlier—as well as the more recent restoration of Williamsburg. She was a member of the City Planning Commission of Little Rock when she found out in 1938 that the houses on the east side of Block 32 were to be torn down. They were in bad condition after being part of the red light district and then being abandoned when the prostitutes were forced out.

She persuaded her friend Max Mayer to come to Little Rock from San Antonio to be the architect for the restoration project. Then she appointed a committee, and finally looked for a source of funding. This resulted in a trip to the WPA administrator, Floyd Sharp. He said her project wasn't what his agency was formed to do and said it would take a lot of money just to buy the property, which he was not allowed to do; so she asked how much that would be. He had seen no plans, knew nothing about it and just pulled an amount out of the blue, $30,000, which he thought was an impossible figure and agreed to take on the work if she raised it. He also said it should be in the hands of a government agency. In writing her formal request she hit on the idea that the Grog Shop had been a meeting place for the legislature, as mentioned in Pope's Early Days of Arkansas, making Arkansas a state of three Capitols. It was not true, as she well knew; but it was a theme for the campaign, and it was documented

Mrs. Loughborough then went to each member of the legislature and said, " I want 30 seconds of your time." She read a typed statement about the restoration, and 30 seconds later she thanked him and was gone. One member said that she was so sweet and considerate that she deserved to get what she asked for, and they appropriated the money, despite the depression. She went back to Mr. Sharp and had the $30,000 to buy the property. At first he didn't remember what she was talking about. Then he realized that he had given his word, never dreaming she could get that large a sum of money; so he had to take funds from other projects to fulfill his promise and allocated $37,000 for labor and supplies for the Territorial Restoration. It opened in July 1941. If it hadn't been for Louise Loughborough, Block 32 would now be a parking lot.

Sour Cream Peach Pie

2 cups peeled, chopped peaches $^3/_4$ cup sugar   2 Tbs. flour

1 cup sour cream   1 egg, beaten $^1/_4$ tsp. each of vanilla and almond extract
Pinch of salt

Combine all ingredients and spoon into a 9" pastry lined pie pan. Bake at 350 degrees 30 to 35 minutes until custard is set. Sprinkle with topping and cook 10 minutes longer.

Topping: Cream together $^1/_4$ cup butter, $^1/_3$ cup brown sugar, $^1/_3$ cup flour, $^1/_2$ tsp. nutmeg, $^1/_4$ tsp. cinnamon, and $^1/_4$ tsp. cloves.

FOSTER A. VINEYARD was born in 1904, and MARGARET CAMPBELL VINEYARD was born in 1911. During World War II, Foster sent a weekly letter to all the soldiers from Little Rock. He carried a small notebook with him at all times and recorded everywhere he went, whom he saw, and what was going on at home. The newsletter was mimeographed on legal size yellow paper; and there were often two sheets, written on both sides. It was a great service because Little Rock was a small town and everybody knew (or knew of) almost everybody else. He was an insurance executive, a member of the Boathouse and was instrumental in the expansion of Little Rock Junior College to a four-year school.

Sweet Potato Pie

1 $^1/_2$ cups cooked sweet potatoes or 1 large can (drained)

Pinch salt   1 Tbs. vanilla   1 cup sugar

1 stick butter, melted   4 egg yolks (save whites) $^1/_3$ cup milk (Milnot or Pet)

$^1/_2$ tsp. baking powder $^1/_2$ tsp. nutmeg

Mix all ingredients well; pour into unbaked pie shell. Bake at 400 degrees for 30 minutes. (If you desire, you can beat saved egg whites with a pinch of cream of tartar to top the pie and let it brown; and you can also add shredded coconut on top of this meringue.)

THOMAS WILLOUGHBY NEWTON, born in Virginia in 1804, was an early citizen of Arkansas Territory and the only Whig elected to Congress from the state. He was also president of The Temperance Society––which caused the newspaper to report the fact that during one hard fought election, Newton, along with others, had fallen off the wagon "in a somewhat spectacular manner."

Brandy Alexander Cream Pie

1 envelope unflavored Knox gelatin	1 cup cold water
2/3 cup sugar	1/8 tsp. salt
3 eggs separated	1 cup cognac
1/4 cup crème de cacao	2 cups heavy cream
1 9" graham cracker crust	Chocolate curls for garnish

Sprinkle gelatin over cold water in saucepan. Stir. Add 1/3 cup sugar, salt, and egg yolks. Stir. Heat over low until it dissolves and thickens – do not boil. Remove. Add cognac and crème de cacao. Chill until mixture starts to mound slightly. Beat whites until stiff. Gradually beat in remaining sugar and fold into thickened mixture. Fold in one cup of whipped cream. Fill crust. Chill overnight. Cover with rest of whipped cream. Garnish with chocolate curls and fine chocolate bits made with a vegetable peeler.

Sheila's Smash Hit

2 cans crushed pineapple

6 oz. miniature marshmallows

1 pint cream, whipped stiff

1/2 cup Grand Marnier or rum

1 can pineapple chunks

1/4 cup of rum

1/2 cup of brown sugar

1/2 cup of pecan halves

The day before, drain the pineapple and stir in marshmallows and 1/4 cup rum. Stir all together and add cream. Refrigerate.

The day of party, caramelize brown sugar in Grand Marnier or rum. (Boil hard until it begins to thicken.) Add pecan halves and cook a few minutes; then spread to cool and separate nuts. When ready to serve, spoon the cream mixture into a shallow bowl, leaving many hills and valleys and sprinkle the nuts about. You may also add drained maraschino cherries. Serves 8 or 9.

(Peg Smith named this low-calorie dessert that tastes calorie-rich for her English friend who gave her the recipe.)

Another early family buried at Mount Holly is the FORSTER clan. The book Jubilee refers to the Forster plots as a "notable example of multi-generational burials;" and their tomb is a sarcophagus. Buried among all these Forsters is EMMA SCREETON FORSTER, born in 1883, who married ROBERT INGERSOLL FORSTER. Emma was one of the true grits who contributed to her family's coffers by writing dime novels. She held a number of positions in pen and press organizations and must have enjoyed it all because she lived 100 years.

Bread Pudding with Whiskey Sauce

3 to 4 slices bread	3 ½ cups milk	4 Tbs. sugar
4 eggs, separated	1 Tbs. vanilla	Pinch salt
Raisins (optional)	½ stick butter	8 level Tbs. sugar

Break bread into ovenproof dish of at least 1 ½ quart capacity. Soften bread with small amount of milk. Beat 4 Tbs. sugar and egg yolks. Add remaining milk and stir well. Add vanilla and salt. Pour milk mixture over bread. Fold in raisins if desired. Dot with butter.

Place dish in pan of water and bake at 300 degrees for 40-50 minutes or until silver knife inserted comes out clean. Remove from oven and raise temperature to 350 degrees. Make meringue using 2 level Tbs. sugar to each egg white. Spread over pudding and return to 350 oven until brown.

Whiskey Sauce:

½ cup sugar	¼ cup water	¼ stick butter
Whiskey to taste		

Cook sugar, water, and butter until butter is melted and sugar dissolved. Remove from heat and add whiskey to taste. Serve with Bread Pudding.

8 servings

Chocolate Dream Dessert

FIRST LAYER:

    1 cup chopped nuts, toasted   1 cup flour   1 stick butter

Mix in 13" x 8" pan and bake ¹/₂ hour at 350 degrees. Stoves vary, so watch to keep from burning. Cool.

SECOND LAYER:

    8 oz. cream cheese   ¹/₂ large Cool Whip   1 cup xxx sugar

    1 tsp. vanilla

Mix cheese and sugar, fold in Cool Whip and vanilla. Cool and chill.

THIRD LAYER:

    2 packages (3 oz.) chocolate instant pudding

Beat with 3 cups milk. Add to pan. Frost with other half of Cool Whip. Sprinkle grated chocolate to decorate. Chill overnight. Freezes well.

Serves 15

(Variations: use 1 package of chocolate pudding and one of vanilla instant pudding or try 2 banana instant puddings.)

FRANZ FORSTER, from Prussia, planned to join his friends—the Anheusers and the Busches—in St. Louis; but when he got as far as Little Rock in 1842, he decided to stay. The public school system, started in 1843, required each pupil to furnish his own desk. Forster made his child's school desk, a wonderful object, obviously not made by a craftsman; and that is its charm. You can see it today at the Historic Arkansas Museum.

The Forsters were pillars of the community, and many are buried at Mount Holly. Their markers are written in English on the front, and in Old German on the back. Appropriately, they all include the words, "AUF WIEDERSEHEN."

INDEX

Pies Puddings & Such

MOUNT HOLLY CEMETERY
ASSOCIATION BOARD OF DIRECTORS

ACKNOWLEDGMENTS

We would like to thank everyone who participated in making this book a reality by submitting recipes and tales of theirs or their relatives. Although most of the photography is by Frances Cranford, we are grateful to the Historic Arkansas Museum, Ron Maxwell of the Governor's Mansion, the Butler Center, and Chris Cranford for special photos.

And to Pat Freeman, the designer, we give our biggest thanks for taking what we had and making it special. We are truly grateful for the gift of her time and talent.

My Favorite Recipes

MY FAVORITE RECIPES

REORDER FORM
To reorder copies of
RECIPES IN PERPETUITY
Contact the Mount Holly Association by mail at:
Mount Holly Cemetery Association
P.O. Box 250118
Little Rock, AR 72225

RECIPES IN PERPETUITY
Timeless Tastes and Tales
from
Residents and Future Residents of Mount Holly

COST:

   $29.95 each

TAX:

   Arkansas residents please add $2.24
   (per book) for sales tax

SHIPPING AND HANDLING:

   1-2 books: $ 5.00, USPS media mail
                $ 7.00, UPS ground
   3-5 books: $ 8.00, USPS media mail
                $10.00, UPS ground
   6-10 books: $12.00, USPS media mail
                $14.00 UPS ground
   (We ship promptly.)

Name _____

Address _____

_____

Phone (_____) _____

Number of books _____ x $29.95 _____

Sales Tax (7.5%, Ark. residents only) _____

Shipping and handling _____

Total: _____

Please make your check payable to "Mount Holly
Cemetery Association" and mail it with this form
to the address above. Thank you.